"What an incredible story of hope and courage. Bob writes with humility and honesty to allow others to see the abundant life of Christ in his son Lucas. We are inspired and challenged by this young man and his family. We believe that Lucas is fulfilling his purpose in life and he 'shines brightly like a star in the sky.' God is truly being glorified through his life. Lucas in his silence is saying, 'Follow me as I follow Christ.'

"Lucas, you are a light showing us the way; thank you for your love and courage."

—MIKE AND CHERYL WELLS
President and Vice President of The Living Center/TLC,
Co-President/Owner of Blue Bunny Foods (Mike)

"This is a life-changing book! We are not the same people after reading this incredible love story. *Light from Lucas* sheds light on the nature of suffering and disappointments, and points us into understanding the magnitude of Love from our Heavenly Father as one human father writes about his love for his son. Thank you, Bob Vander Plaats. Your story has deeply inspired us to live life to the fullest by fulfilling our purpose in this lifetime."

—DR. GARY AND BARB ROSBERG
America's Family Coaches, authors of
The 5 Love Needs of Men and Women

"This inspirational book provides powerful insights about a family's experience in facing challenges and permitting deep faith to help them accept and embrace those challenges."

—ROBERT HOOGEVEEN
Founding CEO of Village Northwest Unlimited

"This story will tug at your heart, then touch your heart, and then touch your soul. It is the real meaning of a Christian family. I truly believe this book should be in every Christian high school's curriculum across this country and should be the basis for an elective course in every private college and university. All churches should make this story part of a young couple's preparation for marriage. I will never have to worry about what wedding present to send to a bride and groom. This story will be our present along with a letter telling how important Christian love and faith are in a marriage and family."

—Bernie Saggau
Former Executive Director,
Iowa High School Athletic Association

"Bob Vander Plaats is known in many ways—as high school principal, businessman, politician—but the role he should perhaps be best known for is his role as father. His dedication to all four of his sons in the midst of such challenging circumstances should remind us all of our greatest duty—providing love for our loved ones. And as he has learned from Lucas, the love returns more than possibly imaginable."

—The Honorable Mike Huckabee
Governor of the State of Arkansas

Light from Lucas

lessons in faith from a fragile life

bob vander plaats

foreword by joni eareckson tada

Tyndale House Publishers, Inc.
Carol Stream, Illinois

A Focus on the Family book published by
Tyndale House Publishers, Inc., Carol Stream, Illinois 60188

TYNDALE and Tyndale's quill logo are registered trademarks of Tyndale House
Publishers, Inc.

Editor: Liz Duckworth
Cover design: Joseph Sapulich
Cover illustration © by Bulent Ince/Istockphoto. All rights reserved.

Library of Congress Cataloging-in-Publication Data
Vander Plaats, Robert.
  Light from Lucas / Bob Vander Plaats.
    p. cm.
  "A Focus on the Family book."
  ISBN-13: 978-1-58997-398-5
  ISBN-10: 1-58997-398-4
  1. Suffering—Religious aspects—Christianity. 2. Lissencephaly—Religious aspects—
Christianity. 3. Vander Plaats, Lucas. 4. Lissencephaly—Patients. 5. Consolation.
I. Title.
  BT732.7.V36 2007
  248.8'63—dc22
                          2006021480

Printed in the United States of America
1 2 3 4 5 6 7 8 9 / 12 11 10 09 08 07

Dedication

Light from Lucas is the result of a life-journey—a life-journey of love. Those on the journey have experienced many peaks and valleys, and some beautiful rainbows. Ironically, we have discovered the true source of light in the darkest times of the journey. Thus this book is dedicated to all the traveling companions on the "Lucas journey." Most specifically, this book is dedicated . . .

to my family

Darla—Lucas's mother—You are the reason we have been allowed to experience the life of Lucas. Your love, your care, and your attention to detail have benefited Lucas with an extended life span that has astounded the educated community. I love you.

Hans, Joshua, and Logan—Lucas's brothers—You have grown to be young men. I have been blessed by the maturity, wisdom, and understanding I have witnessed in each of you that shames most adults, particularly me. I believe God has placed you in front of, alongside of, and behind Lucas for his ongoing protection, care, and love. I love you guys.

and to our angels

Ruth—Lucas's friend—Your servant attitude and genuine love for Lucas and our family is the model for Christian community. Thank you for being part of our family. We love you, Ruth.

Children's Care Hospital and School—Lucas's caregivers. You stand in the gap by caring for and loving Lucas in a selfless and most professional manner. You are a blessing to many children and families. Thanks for making Lucas, and us, feel at home.

Acknowledgments

Kristi Dusenbery

Light from Lucas would not be a reality without the encouragement, guidance, and talent of Kristi Dusenbery. All I can really say is, "thank you." From the very beginning, you affirmed my interest in putting Lucas's story into words. Without your constant and persistent encouragement, *Light from Lucas* would still be a dream.

You are much more than an editor of this book. You are a partner and contributor to its completion. Your prompting, insight, creativity, and talent complement the story of Lucas and have greatly enlightened its life applications.

Focus on the Family

God is awesome! Right from the first concept of putting Lucas's story into a book, I mused with Darla that I would love to see it published with the Focus on the Family seal. Little did I know that this was God's plan . . . right from the beginning.

Focus on the Family inspires me with their authenticity. You have lived up to your billing. Dr. Dobson, Tom Minnery, Larry Weeden, Liz Duckworth, Nanci McAlister, and all the others are steely-eyed focused on the needs and the purpose of the family.

I had goose bumps the first time Larry Weeden told me that Focus on the Family had an interest in publishing *Light from Lucas*. The book is better because of the professional and insightful influence of Liz Duckworth. And *Light from Lucas* is in your hands because of the detailed actions of Nanci McAlister.

Darla and I will strive to reflect the Focus on the Family seal daily!

Joni Eareckson Tada

I was told you don't acknowledge the author of the foreword. I'm not very good at following protocol. Tears filled my eyes, and I got a lump in my throat when I read the words Joni wrote for this book. She has been a valued and constant source of inspiration for people with disabilities and their families.

Besides being an inspiration to Darla and me for years, Joni simply captured the intent of *Light from Lucas*: "inspiring all of us to overcome the hurdles, and discovering God's purpose, in our lives." Thanks, Joni!

Contents

Foreword

I've gotten used to being on display. Whether it's the child study-
ing my wheelchair, the senior citizen across the way smiling sym-
pathetically, or the waiter eyeing me carefully as I use my bent
spoon to eat pieces of hamburger, I'm aware that people are watching. Some might watch out of pity, some out of admiration. All
watch, I sense, with unspoken questions.

It's part of the territory that comes with living in a wheelchair.

It's what Lucas and his family face every day. But like the Vander Plaats family, I choose to think that people's unspoken questions are, for the most part, good-natured. That's because the
author of *Light from Lucas* and I, as followers of Jesus, are con-
strained to think the best of others. We are called to be on display
(as any Christian is). We are encouraged by God's Word to smile
from the inside out as the strength of God shows up bountifully
through our special challenges. When people eye Lucas in his
wheelchair—when people see the smiles on the faces of Bob,
Darla, and their sons, I believe they are thinking, *What an amazing family. How great their God must be to inspire such faith and confidence.*

I'm convinced this is why they chose to tell their story in this
special book. I don't think they mind the fact that their family is
"on display." It's why the book is called *Light from Lucas*. This
young man inspires people who observe him. His entire life—with
all its challenges and struggles—showcases 1 Corinthians 12:24-26,
where we learn that "God has combined the members of the body
and has given greater honor to the parts that lacked it, so that there
should be no division in the body, but that its parts should have

equal concern for each other. If one part suffers, every part suffers with it; if one part is honored, every part rejoices with it."

And I can't help but get a lump in my throat when I think that Lucas's dad decided his son's story was important enough to share—share with people like me and you.

No doubt about it. Your thinking will be illumined by the "light" shared in *Light from Lucas*. You will learn about a family whose hearts are settled and whose peace is profound. Don't worry, though—it's not sugarcoated; there are plenty of hard places with which you'll identify. The most important thing is, you just may end up deciding, *If Lucas can make it and, by the grace of God, overcome his limitations, I can too.*

Joni Eareckson Tada
Joni and Friends International Disability Center
Summer 2006

Chapter One

Expect the Unexpected

"Bob . . . Bob, wake up! We're going to have our baby." Darla's voice was filled with anticipation and excitement as she informed me it was time. This Sunday morning would be the day we would experience the birth of our third child.

We had run this drill twice before—giving birth to two healthy, "normal" boys. Hans was five going on an intellectual fifteen, while Joshua was in the midst of his terrible twos. We felt fully prepared for this baby. Naturally, the baby would have unique personality traits and physical characteristics, but we knew all about the labor and delivery process and the many demands of having a newborn. Although we didn't know the gender of the baby, all our expectations seemed to be in order.

When I was a high school business teacher and basketball coach, I would tell my students of my ambition to have five sons. I joked about my plans to create the perfect basketball team, composed solely of my own genetics. I had already identified Hans as my point guard. He was gifted at handling the ball and had an uncanny feel for the game. Joshua would be my shooting guard. He loved shooting. He also loved kicking, hitting, and anything else that would produce offensive assault on a worthy opponent. Uncles Stan and Jerry were his favorite targets.

This Sunday, June 13, 1993, I was certain Darla would deliver another member of the perfect starting lineup. Maybe he would be a talented forward, the ideal complement to the skill sets of Hans and Josh. I was well on my way to coaching a championship team composed exclusively of my offspring. Wow!

Unfortunately, the plans I teased my students about were quickly thwarted when reality proved far different from light-hearted expectations. Darla did indeed give birth to a son, but thoughts of championship basketball games grew faint as our delivery room drama unfolded.

The baby was breeched in the birth canal, preventing a vaginal delivery. I looked on as doctors and nurses administered an epidural and began cutting into Darla. I looked on as our son was brought harshly into the world, and I looked on as the medical personnel rushed around him with an urgency signaling something very wrong.

His head was abnormally large and completely out of proportion to his frail body. His lips and skin were parched blue, his body craving oxygen. He wasn't pinking-up, a problem that heightened the suspicions of everyone in the room. As I looked on in fear, the doctor took my arm and led me away from the commotion. He had ordered an air ambulance to transport our newborn son from our hometown hospital in Sheldon, Iowa, to a better-equipped hospital in Sioux City. The words he spoke still ring in my head today: "Babies with issues don't belong in rural hospitals."

Issues? What did he mean, "Babies with issues"? This was my baby . . . Darla's baby . . . a future member of the Vander Plaats basketball team. Darla and I were the perfect couple: We started out in the church nursery together; we were kindergarten class-mates and high school sweethearts; we had two normal sons. Now we had a baby with issues? It didn't make any sense. As thoughts whirled through my mind relentlessly, I determined to remain calm outwardly, appearing strong for Darla and those attending our son.

In the midst of this sudden sea of instability, I reached for stability by phoning our parents. This birth announcement was quite unlike those we made with Hans and Josh. It was void of laughter, excitement, and statistical information. Instead, the conversation consisted of stunned reality and requests for help. "Mom, can you stay with Darla at the Sheldon hospital? Dad, can you go with me to St. Luke's in Sioux City? Can you make the necessary phone calls to family and friends? Dan and Beth, can you look after Hans and Josh? Please tell everyone to pray for the son we've yet to hold."

Circumstances were spinning out of control and I was pretending to be strong. Friends, doctors, family members, nurses, strangers, flight technicians, and people requesting signatures came in and out of my confused consciousness, yet I still recall them with vivid detail.

Kissing Darla good-bye, I headed for the van. My dad was with me as I began the one-hour drive to Sioux City. Words are inadequate to describe the intense loneliness I felt as the helicopter carrying our son passed overhead. I was completely helpless. The drive was consumed with rushing thoughts and questions: *I don't even know him. He is my son and I can't do a thing for him. Will he be all right? What went wrong? How is Darla? What about Hans and Josh? What will the future hold? Where is God? What if our baby dies? What if he lives?*

When we reached the hospital we were quickly directed to the neonatal intensive care area. The specialists explained the best-case scenario first, saying our son could just be a big baby, with a big head, struggling to breathe. The optimist in me became hopeful. Then they explained other possibilities. He could have a syndrome that would go undiagnosed for several months. He may have birth defects that could result in a multitude of disabilities. His cranium could be filled with fluid and house almost no brain, resulting in death within weeks or even days. My rising hopes were dashed as I signed for the necessary tests.

Once the tests had begun, the rushing stopped. It was time to catch my breath and begin processing the chaos. After a deep sigh and a moment of prayer, I picked up the phone to call Darla. She was surely experiencing the same numb helplessness. A mother is designed to nurse, bond, and care for her newborn. That normal process had been coldly interrupted with the chopping of helicopter propellers. Now Darla sat in a hospital surrounded by people, but all alone. No Bob. No Hans. No Josh. No baby. She was left with bland walls and recovery procedures, enduring physical and emotional pain.

Our phone conversation was mostly business. We discussed the doctor's information in detail. To the best of my ability, I described the tests that were being performed on our son and we talked about the range of possibilities—from mild to severe disabilities, from normal life to death. Words were sober as our phone call drew to a close, and the question Darla finally asked still sends a chill down my spine as I remember it. "What are we going to do if he's not right?" The emotion in her voice characterized our fear. We were set adrift by the unraveling of the day, and terrified about the future. What began as excited anticipation and predictability had turned into a moment-by-moment battle for composure.

I am rarely at a loss for words, but Darla's question hit me like a ton of bricks and I struggled for an answer. *What will we do if he isn't right?* I paused in silence, remembering my role in this reality drama: *I am the man. I am supposed to be tough. I should be able to handle anything that comes my way.* My voice was quiet and broken as I said, "We'll get through it. We'll get through it."

Dear Lucas,

I love you! I wish I could have expressed my love for you on the day you were born, but the doctors and nurses wouldn't let me near you. And to be honest, I didn't know if I wanted to be close to you at the time.

It still bothers me that your mom and I were not able to appropriately welcome you into the world and into our love and care. Your traumatic birth surprised everyone including Mom and me. We were scared for you and scared for us.

During the nine months that your body was being knit together, you were housed, protected, and nourished by your mom. Just as with Hans and Josh, you and Mom bonded during pregnancy. It is a beautiful process and one of God's greatest gifts to mothers. Mom loved being pregnant and she was good at it.

You need to know that your mom paid attention to every detail during your incubation. She loves to read and read everything she could find to enhance your development in the womb. But regardless of the many pages she read, there weren't any books or warning signs to adequately prepare us for your birth.

God made only one YOU . . . for only one US.

The separation you felt at the time of your birth was a parting from Mom. The separation Mom felt was a parting from you. I didn't feel any immediate separation; I felt confused and disappointed. You were not what I was looking for, and I really didn't know you. You see, dads are spectators in the pregnancy game. Yeah, I enjoyed putting on a good show to convince people that I felt just as pregnant and attached to you as Mom did, but the fact is—I didn't have a clue.

I had no idea how God would use you and your unique abilities to impact my self-absorbed life.

It is a privilege to devote this book to you, Lucas. You have taught me many life-lessons and it is my hope that relaying these lessons will impact the lives of many others.

Thanks for accepting me. Thanks for teaching me. Thanks for loving me. And thanks for bringing so much joy to my life.

"I love Lucas ... I love Lucas. Yes, I do! Yes, I do! He's my buddy, buddy ... buddy, buddy, buddy. I love you ... I love you!"

I do love you, Lucas, more today than the day you were born, more tomorrow than today.

Dad

♪♪   ♪♪   ♪♪   ♪♪   ♪♪   ♪♪   ♪♪   ♪♪   ♪♪   ♪♪

"I Love Lucas" is a song I sing to my son. It fits the tune of "Frère Jacques."

Chapter Two

Make It Count

I was a five-year-old kindergartener, still sleeping in a bed against the back wall of my parents' bedroom. With six kids in the family and one on the way, we were running out of sleeping quarters in our two-story, middle-class home. The bed my oldest brother slept in was curiously positioned in the hallway at the top of the staircase, just above the entryway. Although we were cramped for space, I believe its location had more to do with strategy than necessity, allowing Mom and Dad to keep a close eye on a teenage son in the prime of sowing his wild oats.

My first vivid memory came early one morning, when my dad sat down on my bed to wake me up and deliver some eagerly awaited news: Mom had just given birth to our newest sibling. I remember being instantly excited as I waited for the details. Was it a girl or a boy? What was the baby's name? I was finally a big brother! Instead of giving me the particulars, Dad informed me that I would not be going to school that day. My baby brother had been stillborn—DOA, dead on arrival. The thrill of exciting news was quickly followed by a crushing blow and confused disappointment.

Although the events that followed are less clear to me, I do remember standing at the graveside funeral with my dad and siblings. We were joined by a few friends and relatives and our pastor. Mom was still in the hospital recuperating from childbirth, so she was unable to attend the service. As I stood quietly next to Dad, my eyes moved back and forth between the little white box holding the baby brother I had so anxiously awaited and the tiny void in the ground that would soon become his body's home.

From my earliest memory, I have had cause to contemplate death.

A short time later, I noticed a framed photograph in our living room; it showed a beautiful little girl with dark hair and blue eyes. I remember asking Mom who the girl was and why we had a picture of her. After a long pause, Mom replied, "That is your sister Barbie."

Really? I thought. I didn't even know I had a sister named Barbie.

Mom explained how Barbie had a rare type of kidney disease, and they had traveled with her frequently to the University of Iowa hospital for diagnosis and treatment. In the winter of Barbie's kindergarten year she became ill with flu-like symptoms. Mom suspected the symptoms indicated more than a seasonal virus and took Barbie to the doctor on a Monday. After gathering information concerning her lack of appetite and inability to keep food down, the doctor reasonably concluded that it was merely the flu. Still sensing a bigger issue, they returned to the doctor each day that week only to be sent home time and time again. By Sunday morning, Mom's perseverance won out and Barbie was admitted to the hospital. Sunday afternoon, Christmas day, Barbie died due to heightened complications of her kidney disease brought on by the flu.

Once again at a very young age, I had cause to contemplate death.

By the summer of 1979 I had grown into an "invincible" 16-year-old, enjoying the independence of having my own driver's license. One hot July night, after cruising the streets of our small town in my '67 Buick Skylark, I managed to arrive home right at midnight, just in time to meet my Friday-night curfew.

Brian, my older brother, was already asleep in the room we shared, with the window propped open in hopes of a cool breeze. I slipped into bed and was just dozing off when I heard a car speed into our driveway. The front door flew open, then quickly slammed shut as our oldest and married brother, Stan, ran up the stairs and down the hall to our parents' bedroom. He spoke with great intensity as he told them to wake up and get dressed. He explained that my parents' fourth-oldest child, Harlan (nicknamed Hawk), had been severely injured in a car crash. We needed to get to Sioux Falls, South Dakota, as quickly as possible.

The terror still resonates in my mind today when I force myself to remember the details of those early-morning moments. I climbed into the family car with my mom and dad and brother Brian. Stan arranged for Vern, a family friend, to drive the 70-mile journey for us. It was a quiet ride. My mom was stunned silent, only voicing a few deep sighs and an occasional cry of "why" in prayer.

My dad was the man. Clearly he was concerned about the condition of his son, but he remained remarkably composed, a source of strength for the rest of us. Little did I know that his example would prove to be precious when I faced the fear of losing my own son years later.

Dad asked Vern to tell him the details. How did the accident happen? Who was involved? How were the others doing?

Vern's answers made us all aware of the accident's seriousness. Harlan's girlfriend and the other female passenger had been taken to a local hospital, and both were expected to make full recoveries. Vern explained that Dennis, the driver of the car, was "no longer with us." Dennis and Harlan had both been on the driver's side of the vehicle, which absorbed the fatal blow of the collision. The statement, "He's no longer with us," rendered all other details of the accident insignificant. All we were told about Harlan was that he was found unresponsive at the scene but was still breathing on his own. He was in trouble.

After we finally arrived at the hospital, our family gathered in the intensive care waiting area. We didn't know what to think or how to act. The doctor arrived to inform us there was little hope for recovery of any kind. Harlan's brain stem looked as if it had been cut with a knife due to the whiplash force of the impact. He was holding on by a very thin thread.

Harlan hung on by that thread for five days. Our family rode the waves from hope to despair. At times we prayed, "Please allow him to live," and other times we prayed, "Please take him quickly." The waiting area had become our home since the time of the accident, and on the fifth day our entire family was called to gather by Harlan's bedside.

The timing of this request seemed ironic, since it came almost immediately after Mom and Dad had returned to the waiting area with renewed hope and optimism. Each night they would go together, just the two of them, to say a prayer at Harlan's bedside. Mom would hold his hand as Dad prayed for divine intervention and for God's will to be done. On this night, Harlan squeezed Mom's hand and pulled it over his heart. What we had interpreted as cause for optimism was actually his way of affirming his love— and saying good-bye.

Nevertheless, when the nurses suggested that the family should gather in his room, we did not question them. We moved quickly to my brother's hospital bed, working our way around monitors and life-support equipment. Our family held hands as my oldest brother offered a prayer. When he ended his prayer with "Amen," the repetitive beeping of the heart monitor became a single tone and the screen revealed a straight line. It was a moment of comfort I will always hold dear, for at that very moment we knew Harlan had transitioned from his earthly home to his heavenly one.

At the invincible age of 16, I again had cause to contemplate death.

The deaths of my three siblings have had a major impact on my life. We cannot know when, where, or how we are going to die. The only certainty is that death is certain; the mortality rate is still holding at 100 percent.

Though the reality of their lives and deaths has given me much to ponder, it is Lucas's life that has taught me about the incredible frailty of our existence. Right from his first breath he has been teetering on the bridge between life and death, existing in a whirl-wind of watchful eyes and medical equipment.

By his fifteenth month, I had been called on twice to revive Lucas, performing rescue breathing while 9-1-1 was called. Both times resulted in emergency helicopter rides, and both times I was reminded of the great importance of counting his days, giving thanks for every moment. Soon after these experiences I promised myself to do everything in my power to make his life count regardless of its certain brevity.

As a result of these episodes, doctors determined his condition to be seizure related. They modified his medications and prescribed food supplements for weight gain. Lucas rallied quickly and became quite healthy despite his odd exterior. His large head, way out of proportion to his frail body, even prompted one of our son's friends to refer to Lucas as "E.T." Though the comment was hurtful, it was an accurate description of his appearance.

By the time he reached 15 months, he was averaging a life-flight every 5 months. Though this is not a desirable statistic, it was the only thing he had on his brothers, who thought riding in a helicopter would be very cool.

It was following the second helicopter emergency, when Lucas was still an infant, that Darla and I were confronted with a question we had not been asked before. Once Lucas had been stabilized in the intensive care unit and connected to all the proper equipment, the doctors asked: "If Lucas stops breathing or begins deteriorating in condition, do you want us to implement lifesaving measures, or would you rather we just make him comfortable?" We were taken aback by the reality of his words, but the answer came quickly for both of us. "Revive him."

Once again, I had cause to contemplate death. Darla and I began discussing death with sobering frequency—specifically, Lucas's death.

When I was a high school principal in Sheldon, we lived in a home near the local cemetery. Frequently, after a long day at school, I would go on a walk. It helped me process the day's events and prepare for upcoming meetings and activities. These walks inevitably took me through the beautifully quiet cemetery pathways, where the stars seemed brighter and the colors more vivid.

The sound of my footsteps was humbling as I walked and studied the tombstones. I noticed some told tales of long and full existences, while others reflected abbreviated lives, lives which seemed way too short. I would walk along surveying the name, date of birth, date of death, epitaph, and other unique characteristics written on each tombstone as I tried to gain a glimpse into each person's life.

My walks usually progressed to the west side of the cemetery along Union Avenue where I would stop and reflect on the gravesites of my three siblings. There were Harlan, Barbie, and my baby brother Bradley. As I studied their names, I thought of how great it would be to have them there with me—laughing, talking, knowing one another's spouses and children. Then I would think, *Let me get this straight. They are in heaven and I want them in Sheldon?* My conclusion was always the same. I was being selfish.

One day, after hearing a message by famed football coach Lou Holtz,[1] I was inspired to view the tombstones of that cemetery in an entirely new way. They were all very similar, with one symbolic difference—the dash. Each grave marker had the same statistical elements, but the dash placed between the date of birth and the date of death represented each person's contribution to life. I began to view the dash as a symbol of the impact each person had in his or her abundance or lack of time on earth. Since that day, my focus has changed from contemplating the number of days, to the impact of days. Whether we are given one minute or one hundred years, God intends for each of us to make a contribution.

Lucas's days may not be as many or as normal as we would like, but I am confident that they have been purposeful. His life has inspired me to seek my own purpose with passion and to motivate others to do the same. Lucas has taught me the importance of living my "dash" to its fullest.

Are you determined to make your dash count? Maybe you are thinking, *What could I possibly contribute? I'm not a gifted poet like Shakespeare, a humanitarian like Mother Teresa, or a genius like Einstein. I just get up each day, take care of business, and try to stay out of trouble.* True. Maybe some lives are less public and profound than others, but no life is without significance.

Ephesians 2:10 says, "For we are God's workmanship, created in Christ Jesus to do good works, which God prepared in advance for us to do." God has a purpose for every human life. He has planned for you to do things no one else can do.

The significance doesn't lie in the grandiosity of our contribution, but in the heart of it. If you are called to be at home with your children, you must do it with passion. If you are called to start your own business, you must do it with passion. If you are called to teach, you must do it with passion. Whatever you are called to do, you must do it with passion! There will always be someone who is more talented or better prepared, but Psalm 139:13-14 reminds us: "For you [God] created my inmost being; you knit me together in my mother's womb. I praise you because I am fearfully and wonderfully made." He designed each of us perfectly, with all we need to accomplish that which He has planned for us.

Some may look at Lucas and wonder what purpose he could possibly fulfill, but he too is fearfully and wonderfully made with everything he needs to complete his calling. He cannot walk, or read, or speak. He will never be a doctor, or a lawyer, or a father. He requires full-time care to meet his physical needs. Yet he has a unique and significant purpose that only he can fulfill. His "dash" is making an impact.

Contemplating death may be necessary at times, but it is far better to contemplate life! Dream big and search for your significance relentlessly. You didn't choose the day you were born, you cannot know how many days you have before you will die, but you can determine how you will live today.

Make the decision to laugh more often, take more risks, love more deeply, complain less, help a neighbor, offer a kind word, clean up a mess that isn't yours, forgive someone, say "I'm sorry," say "thank you," pray for a friend, pray for a stranger, learn something new, set a new goal. Little by little, the choices you make today are writing your story. Whether you're given a few more hours or many more years, choose to make a difference, to live your "dash" with passion and make every moment count.

Dear Lucas,

Your life has taught me so much.

I love to cruise with you. It is priceless to see your face as you sit in the copilot's chair anticipating the start of the engine. I get so much joy from watching your excitement as the car's engine starts and the music begins to play. I love it when you clap your chest, stiffen your body, and sing in your own beautiful way to the music.

When you settle into the ride and relax, the squint of your nose, the wrinkles by your eyes, and the coo in your voice tell me you feel blessed. The little things—yeah, the little things—are what give you joy. Because of you, they give me joy too. Thanks for reminding me of life's simple pleasures!

If it were up to me, I would remove all of your disabilities. You would have no more pain. You would have no more fear. You would walk. You would run. You would play. You would be completely healthy. More than anything, you would talk. You would share your thoughts, your hopes, your fears, and your dreams.

The irony in my wishes is that I would be robbing your life of God's purpose. Your life, your near-death experiences, your pain, your seizures, and your disabilities all have had a positive impact on many lives. Because of you, others have been drawn closer to God and have been challenged to discover their purposes.

I'm sure you notice that some people don't really know how to respond to you. Some, either verbally or nonverbally, question your existence because you don't look "normal" to them. Our "Victoria's Secret" world of bodily perfection isn't *made for you and, on many levels, you can be really thankful for this.*

It may not be easy, but don't worry about those who are unwilling to embrace your uniqueness. Instead, focus on those people who are inspired by it!

Hans writes your name on the inside of his basketball shoes as a reminder that any challenge he may face pales in comparison to your daily obstacles. Mom and I have moved and changed careers to maximize the impact of our lives and your life, according to God's perfect will.

Your life has motivated others to maximize their impact here on earth. More so, your life encourages others to contemplate the Creator. Don't ever forget that your life has a unique purpose, Lucas.

I thank God for your life and I thank you for living it with passion!

Dad

Chapter Three

It Could Be Worse

What is my problem? Why am I so sad? Not only do I lack joy, I feel deprived—robbed of luxuries that are found in others' lives and tired of living with situations that seem so unfair. Sound familiar? At age 32, I found myself asking these questions, feeling angry and discouraged.

For years Darla and I have had a typical Sunday-morning drill. We corral the kids in the car, arriving at church with just enough time to offer a few greetings before taking our seats in our favorite pew. After the service the boys make their way to their Sunday school classes, while Darla and I go to our class, grabbing a cup of coffee and a pastry on the way. One such Sunday, we were visiting with friends in the hallway after class, waiting for Hans and Josh to rejoin us. Darla was holding Lucas and talking with a group of women, while I discussed the previous night's game with Dave, Bruce, and Denny. All at once Darla motioned to me, her face dressed in fear. Fifteen-month-old Lucas was turning blue; he wasn't breathing. I scooped him up and rushed to an empty classroom to begin rescue-breathing measures, asking a friend to call 9-1-1.

By the time the ambulance arrived, Lucas was breathing, but his breaths were shallow and labored.

The emergency room was a flurry of activity when we arrived, and we could hear the nurse hollering, "It's Lucas!" He had developed quite a reputation in his short time on earth.

The doctors were able to get him stabilized, but they wanted to fly him to a hospital in Sioux Falls, South Dakota, for further treatment and observation. Darla accompanied Lucas in the helicopter, while I stayed in Sheldon long enough to get Hans and Josh delivered to family members.

In the quiet hours driving to Sioux Falls in our van, I was consumed with thoughts of *Why me? Why Lucas? Why our family?* I was focused on myself and indulging in a pity that seemed well-warranted. Why couldn't we just enjoy a normal Sunday morning, like everyone else?

Arriving at the hospital, I found my way to the intensive care room. Darla and Lucas were there with the doctor, and I was given an assessment of Lucas's condition. As the doctor concluded his update, he asked the question that had become soberly familiar: "If the events of this morning are repeated in this hospital room in Sioux Falls, do you want us to implement lifesaving measures to save Lucas?"

Our answer remained the same: "Of course, we want you to revive him." The doctor's question was not a new one, but it struck me with new emotion. It seemed as though he was questioning the worth of Lucas's life. Was it a life worth saving?

The recent months had drawn me close to mental collapse. We had been through more than a year of uncertainty with Lucas, while still trying to raise our other two sons and maintain a sense of normalcy in our home. Some brand of breakdown seemed to be looming and this latest visit to the ICU produced an insatiable need to catch my breath. I had convinced myself that I was not allowed the privilege of showing emotion. Darla and the boys needed to see a strong husband and father, able to stay composed and in control.

As I stepped out of Lucas's room, I glanced into the room of another little boy, and my selfish thoughts were quickly diverted. This preschooler didn't appear to have a physical or mental disability. He didn't appear to have breathing problems or a seizure disorder. In fact, he appeared to be completely normal. This little boy was apparently healthy, but he sat in the intensive care unit crying out in pain because someone had used a cigarette as a means of discipline, burning his flesh from the top of his head to the soles of his little feet.

God used that scene to crash my pity party in dramatic fashion, and the message was loud and clear: It could be so much worse. When I was a preschooler, sleeping in a crib in my parents' room, self-preservation was never a concern. My parents always cared for me, always protected me, and always loved me. My home was a place of safety, never one of fear.

Regardless of Lucas's fragile condition, his experience with invasive medical procedures, his inability to participate in normal boyhood activities, and his constant fight for survival, at least we could be certain that he was loved. Darla and I, his brothers, grandparents, extended family, and many family friends surrounded him with love and kindness. His well-being had always been a priority.

Still standing in the hospital hallway, my mind drifted to my experiences as a high school principal, when I witnessed too many teenagers becoming parents—children having children. I contemplated the life of Lucas in the hands of a teenage mother or in the hands of an abusive father. My heart cried out in repentance. *It could be worse.*

I was suddenly filled with gratitude that Lucas did indeed belong to me, to our family. God seemed to be saying, "Quit whining and hold your head up. Get things into perspective, and get on with life."

At family gatherings, my older brother Brian is often heard saying, "What about me?" He wants us to pay attention to him. Now, if you think that is odd behavior for a man in his forties, you're right. Nevertheless, it always gets a laugh, gaining him the attention he desires.

Most of us have not made a habit of verbalizing the question, "What about me?" But we ask it repeatedly through our attitudes and actions. We are flooded with vanity every time we turn on the television or look at a magazine. "You owe it to yourself." "If it feels good, do it." "Have it your way." Our society puts a priority on self-indulgence, convincing us that we must satisfy our own needs for happiness before we will ever be able to please others.

We are a long way from the attitude President Kennedy expressed when he admonished his fellow Americans to "ask not what your country can do for you. Ask what you can do for your country."[2] Instead, we have become more about receiving than giving. We have become obsessed with self-gratification and the accumulation of material possessions.

The danger of putting a priority on personal fulfillment is addressed very directly in Luke 12:16-21. Jesus tells the tale of a farmer with a bumper crop. The man's land produces such a large crop that he has no place to store the excess, so he decides to tear down his barns and build bigger barns. Seems logical, doesn't it? He boasts that he has enough food to last many years, ensuring a carefree future. Though it seems logical, even responsible, God calls him a fool and explains that he will die long before he is able to enjoy what he has accumulated.

If Jesus would have ended the tale there, it might lead us to assume that God is against wealth and responsible planning for the future. But that wasn't the end of the story. The last sentence of Luke 12 reveals the message: "This is how it will be with anyone who stores up things for himself but is not rich toward God." God is not displeased with possessions, but He is passionate about priorities. When we spend more time and energy making our lives comfortable here on earth than we spend seeking a relationship with God, we are fools.

God wants us to take the focus off of ourselves and become consumed with Him. He wants us to seek His face before we trace His hand. If the farmer had sought the face of God, rather than seeking security in material abundance, he might have realized that there was far more joy and fulfillment to be gained by blessing those around him.

After telling the story of the farmer, Jesus says, "But seek his kingdom, and these things will be given to you as well. Do not be afraid, little flock, for your Father has been pleased to give you the kingdom. Sell your possessions and give to the poor. Provide purses for yourselves that will not wear out, a treasure in heaven that will not be exhausted, where no thief comes near and no moth destroys. For where your treasure is, there your heart will be also" (Luke 12:31-34).

God doesn't promise us wealth, life without struggle, or children born without disabilities. He simply wants us to remember that He has already given us everything. When Jesus died and rose again to save us from our sin, He gave us the kingdom, an eternal treasure that cannot be stolen or destroyed. Jesus' words in the above passage are a gentle reminder that our focus (for where your treasure is) will determine our happiness (there your heart will be also).

I believe that God was speaking to me that day in the hospital hallway, reminding me to major in the majors and to seek Him first. Lucas will never bring home a bumper sticker that says "My Kid Is on the Honor Roll." We will never hear the crowd cheer for

him as he makes a game-winning shot. He will never captivate an
audience with musical talent. But when he hears me sing "I love
Lucas, I love Lucas," his face shines with a smile that fills my heart
with immeasurable joy. That is what I treasure. I must determine
to be so swept away with what he is able to do, that his deficiencies become secondary.

In the eyes of this world, Lucas's contribution to life could be
better. But it could also be worse. Our journey with Lucas has
challenged us to continually evaluate our perspective. Throughout
this book we talk at length about focus and perspective. You may
be thinking, "Okay, I've got it!" But do you? Do you make it
through a week or a day without worrying or complaining about
a difficult circumstance? Are you focused on temporal pleasures or
eternal rewards? Do you spend more time blessing others than
seeking your own pleasure? Do your attitudes and actions reflect
an understanding that it could be worse?

Parents often ask their children, "How many times do I have
to tell you . . . ?" I suppose our heavenly Father could ask each of
us the same question, yet His patience and grace are unmatched.
He wants us to be satisfied and to trust Him completely, yet we fail
over and over again. We feel deprived. We get stuck in a state of
discouragement. And we question God's plan. Just as parents use
consequences to shape the character of their children, God uses the
situations of our lives to make us stronger and to remind us that
this life is temporary.

It saddens me to think of what God must have thought as He
observed my pity party the day I drove to the Sioux Falls hospital.
If He had been there in flesh, I imagine He may have challenged
me by saying, "I love Lucas more than you ever could. He is My
son too. Please stop concentrating on your perceived injustice, and
simply trust Me. Focus on what you do have. You have the oppor-

tunity to hold him, to watch him clap his hands, and to laugh with him. Having Lucas is helping you understand My sufficiency and depend on it, because it has made you painfully aware of your own insufficiency. You are learning that grumbling about your situation won't change a thing. Bob, it isn't a perfect life that will make your joy complete, but a perfect God. Someday Lucas will be fully restored, but today he is yours to love—just as he is."

When I ran for governor of the state of Iowa, I participated in several debates with my fellow candidates. These situations could be quite intimidating. Often unexpected questions would be asked by panelists and occasionally by opponents. The lights were bright and hot. There were reporters, cameras, and microphones surrounding us. I knew I must be flawless in order to gain needed support, and every eye in the room seemed to be staring right at me.

Every time I participated in a debate, I placed a photograph of Lucas on my podium. Following one such event an opponent inquired about the photo. I explained that seeing a picture of Lucas reminded me that things really aren't so bad. The worst thing that could possibly happen while campaigning wouldn't compare with what Lucas must endure every day. It reminded me that my situation could be worse.

Companies spend millions of dollars convincing us we need new cars, nicer houses, and perfect children in order to be happy. Sadly, we often believe it. But how would our attitudes be different if we reminded ourselves daily that it could be worse? When our boys are running and screaming through the house, getting on our nerves, Darla and I thank God that they can speak and that they have legs that work.

Looking at Lucas causes me to ask the question, "What is my problem?" He has taught me to make every day a good day. I can walk and run. I can talk and sing. My body is healthy. Lucas has given me a fresh appreciation for my abilities and has inspired me to give more of myself, my talents, my resources, and my energy. He has taught me that things could be so much worse. He has taught me that true joy is only found when I surrender my desires and frustrations, fully trusting God's sufficiency, and focus diligently on the blessings in my life.

♦ ♦   ♦ ♦   ♦ ♦   ♦ ♦   ♦ ♦   ♦ ♦   ♦ ♦   ♦ ♦   ♦ ♦

Dear Lucas,

You've been through so much: five helicopter rides, three resuscitations, a few code blues, countless seizures, and one major surgery. You have a tracheotomy to help you breathe and the doctors have talked about giving you a feeding tube.

For all of your 13 years on this earth you've been unable to walk, run, read, or talk. In addition to these physical and medical limitations, you live away from home and don't have the opportunity to experience daily life with your family on a regular basis.

According to many people's standards, your life condition could not be worse. But before you go thinking, "Duh," and begin having a pity party, I want you to focus on what you do have.

You live in a great country. Your doctors, nurses, educators, therapists, and caregivers are among the best in the world. You are alive and experiencing a great quality of life because of America's expertise, generosity, and compassion.

You are surrounded by and engulfed in love. I love you. Mom loves you. Your brothers love you. Your grandpas and grandmas love you. Your uncles and aunts love you and Ruth loves you. Most importantly, God loves you!

Because of this love, your needs will always be met. And because of this love, you have everything!

Time and time again, I've seen you bring out the best in others. In evaluating life, I don't believe that we will be measured according to what we accomplished for ourselves, but according to what we have done for others. And based on that measurement, you are living a great life!

Lucas, don't ever forget that your life could be worse. You have the best of care, the best of love, and you bring out the best in others. Above all, you have hope. The God who created and loves you will someday welcome you into heaven with the gift of a perfect body, full of glory and power. That will be an awesome day!

As I've told you before, you are not the child I prayed for but I am so thankful you are the child I received. You have taught me to appreciate the "things" in life that have eternal value, and for that I am eternally grateful.

Keep on being a blessing, Lucas! I love you.

Dad

❧ ❧   ❧ ❧   ❧ ❧   ❧ ❧   ❧ ❧   ❧ ❧   ❧ ❧   ❧ ❧   ❧ ❧   ❧ ❧

"So will it be with the resurrection of the dead. The body that is sown is perishable, it is raised imperishable; it is sown in dishonor, it is raised in glory; it is sown in weakness, it is raised in power; it is sown a natural body, it is raised a spiritual body. If there is a natural body, there is also a spiritual body." (1 Corinthians 15:42-44)

Chapter Four

Don't Wear Masks

Arthur Fonzarelli . . . Fonzie . . . the Fonz. He was the great role model and fashion icon of my adolescence. Fonzie was cool.

In the spring of 1977 I was in eighth grade and my track team was participating in a multi-school meet at Northwestern College in Orange City, Iowa. Track athletes dressed differently in 1977 than they do today. We didn't wear full warm-ups or carry matching duffel bags. Instead, we boarded the track bus in blue jeans and jean jackets because we were trying to be cool . . . like Fonzie.

Our team arrived at the college and took its place on the field inside the track where we would wait for our chosen events to be announced. When I heard the call for the high jump, I removed my jean jacket to expose my Sheldon Christian Meteors jersey, something I was very proud to wear, and began preparing for the event.

As I finished a series of stretches, standing among my teammates, I removed my blue jeans. About that time, there was a roar of laughter. Being distracted, I had missed the joke, but laughed anyway because that's what middle schoolers do: Even if you don't know why they're laughing, when your friends laugh, you laugh. So I was enjoying the moment until Fred said, "Hey, Bob, you forgot your shorts!"

There I stood in my chosen underwear for the day! But, just like Fonzie, I stayed cool.

After pulling my jeans back on, I found our coach and explained my dilemma. He quickly grabbed an extra pair of shorts from his bag, shoved them into my arms, and sent me running to the locker room to change.

As soon as I pulled the shorts up around my waist, I knew I had a problem. They were at least three sizes too big and were never going to stay on my waist, especially during a high-jump competition!

"Last call for the high jump" came booming over the loudspeaker. I rushed back to my coach, who proceeded to wrap the waistband of my shorts—Johnny's shorts—with athletic tape.

I still can't believe I let him do that! Despite all the excitement, I made it to the high jump in time to compete and was doing surprisingly well. In fact, I made it to the final group of three and was preparing to attempt a jump that would beat my personal best.

As I prepared, I spotted Rhonda. Rhonda was a high jumper from another team, and Rhonda was a babe! If I could clear the bar and keep my shorts up, I might have a shot with her. It was a true "wonder years" moment.

I concentrated. I visualized a successful jump. Adrenaline rushed through my body as I ran the path and approached the bar. As soon as my feet left the ground, I knew I was going to make it. It was the best jump of my life. I cleared the bar by a couple of inches and the tape around my waist stayed intact. Rhonda was as good as mine. Regrettably, I jumped too close to the corner, flew past the landing mat, and my body slammed onto the asphalt track. I was bloody, with black tar embedded in my backside. But just like Fonzie, I stayed cool.

Everyone was looking at me, watching me, and talking about my ridiculous landing. My chances with Rhonda were definitely done.

Looking back over the years, I realize the opinions of others have always mattered a great deal to me—specifically, their opinions about me. One of the traditions our society has established is the insincerity with which we ask the question, "How are you?" when passing an acquaintance or even a stranger. In theory, it's a great question. It has the potential to help us gain true insight into the life of another—insight that might be used to build a friendship, offer a helping hand, or share a word of encouragement.

However, asking this question has become nothing more than a formality. And so have the answers. "Fine, thanks." "I'm great . . . how 'bout you?" Never mind the pain in our marriage. Forget about the fear of the pending test results or the financial stress of being unemployed. We give brief, predictable answers because that's what the world wants to hear.

People want to hear that we are good, great, or even awesome. We hide our concerns and struggles because we don't want others to think less of us. Whether we are five or fifty, we don't want our deficiencies to show because we want people to believe we have it all together.

When I was young, boys were taught to act tough. We weren't supposed to cry when we fell off our bikes or scraped our knees. We learned to buck up because the world doesn't want weak boys. The only time it was okay to cry was during or after sporting events. Otherwise we were to maintain a tough exterior at all times.

Early in life boys and girls alike learn to be very selective about who sees their weaknesses. When a child gets injured, the reaction is likely to be far more dramatic if Mom is the only witness than if the child is on the playground with friends. Why? We let Mom hear us wail because she will love us despite our failures, but we act tough for our friends so they won't laugh at us or think we're stupid for getting hurt. We decide early in life that it's easier to hide our deficiencies than to risk being judged for them.

Have you ever wanted to say how you really felt but simply said, "fine"? Have you ever said yes, even though you wanted to say no? Do you listen to different types of music depending on who is around you? Do you attend certain activities simply to fit in? By the way, these are not just questions for kids. They are questions for adults too.

Our lives become consumed with attending the right social gatherings, driving the right vehicles, and having the right jobs. We want our kids to be mature and achieve good grades so people will think we are good parents. We learn that it is safer to live socially acceptable, politically correct lives than to risk being unpopular. And we learn to judge our success by the world's standards: *How much power do I have? How much prestige do I have? How many possessions have I accumulated?*

When I am introduced as the Founder and President of MVP Leadership, it gives me a sense of accomplishment. When I ran for governor, I developed a great sense of prestige. When Darla and I had our new home built, it was a possession of which we were very proud. In many ways, I have allowed things like these to define me. As a matter of fact, I like having these things define me because I want people to think highly of me. I want them to know me by my success, not by failures or mediocrity.

To some degree it matters to each of us what other people think. It matters what others think of our careers and our social circles. It matters what others think of our spouses and our kids. It matters what others think of our vehicles and the positions we hold in the community. It matters. And it causes us to become masters of disguise, wearing whatever mask the situation dictates. We accumulate a complex collection of masks, each one designed to protect the core of who we really are. Each one is designed to showcase our power, prestige, or possessions so our inadequacies will remain neatly tucked away.

I habitually wore masks for many years. When in the business arena, I sported the mask of a leader. At church, I sported the mask of godly husband and father. When coaching a basketball game, I sported the mask of a motivator. In fact, I became an expert at masquerading and was quite content with my mask collection—until Lucas entered our lives.

Lucas has a head that is much larger than normal. His hair is patchy in places and he has very low muscle tone. Lucas has frequent seizures. He cries out when he's happy and he cries out when he's sad. There is no hiding his disabilities, his deficiencies. No matter the party he attends or the home he visits, Lucas is Lucas.

The beauty of Lucas is that he never wears masks. He will cry out when it is inappropriate to cry out. He will laugh when it is inappropriate to laugh. He will clap when it is inappropriate to clap. And he will demand an emergency helicopter ride even when it disrupts our lives. He is real. He doesn't pretend to think or feel a particular way in order to please others. He doesn't even know how to pretend. That is what makes him so attractive to me. He defines authenticity.

From the time Lucas was born, people have wanted to know how we are doing and how Lucas is doing. We are often asked the habitual question, "How are you?" Although we appreciate the inquiries, we realize that most people don't really want to take the time necessary to hear the details of our life with Lucas.

For more than a year we gave tidy answers, answers that took 10 seconds or less and answers that ensured the comfort of those inquiring. As time passed, though, I had a growing desire to give candid answers, to be authentic. In the fall of 1994, we allowed our local newspaper to publish a front-page story about Lucas's world. We talked very openly about the impact Lucas's life was having on Hans and Josh. We talked about our hopes and dreams for Lucas and how Darla and I felt when he was diagnosed with Partial Pachygyria Lissencephaly. The opportunity to be authentic was refreshing. We were finally able to give the lengthy, honest, and sometimes uncomfortable answers to the question, "How are you doing?"

Lucas was born two days after the birth of Jacob, Darla's nephew. Jake gave us an immediate means of comparison, a constant reminder of the expectation for boys Lucas's age. Jake was born healthy. He has grown to be a great kid with a charming personality. He is extremely competitive and has won awards at several basketball camps. We realized right away that Lucas would never measure up to Jake. Not only was it disheartening to compare the two, I am convinced that it was a disservice to Lucas, to Darla and me, and even to Jake to do so.

That is why, when we were interviewed for the newspaper article, I talked about the way we had come to assess Lucas's progress. Early in his life, we stopped comparing him to other children his age and began measuring him to the likes of a cross-country runner. A good cross-country runner understands that he is running every race against himself. His success depends on meeting and improving his own best times.

We began comparing Lucas to Lucas. Is he beating his personal best? Is he attaining that which he is able to attain according to the abilities God has given him?

When Lucas was seven years old we attended a staffing that I will never forget. We sat around a table with several professionals prepared to give their assessments of our son. They took turns, each one describing the age level Lucas had reached in a particular category. They systematically discussed his physical and cognitive development. Yet I was concerned that not one of them even mentioned our son's capacity for contentment. Not one of them addressed his level of happiness. Parents want to know their children are happy. We want our children to feel fulfilled, to find success according to their unique God-given talents and gifts. Nobody was telling me that Lucas was happy.

I waited for them to go through their extensive studies before calling a proverbial time-out. I explained that I cared deeply about his progress, but more importantly, I wanted to know that he was happy. I asked them if there was some sort of "happiness continuum."

Lucas will never be a rocket scientist. He will never walk and, unless there is a miracle, he will never talk. Even though we would love that to happen, we are convinced it won't, and I wanted this room of professionals to understand that his emotional well-being is our greatest concern. At that moment charts and graphs measuring Lucas's progress against societal standards seemed cold and senseless.

It felt as though they were judging his worth according to the way he stacked up against others. They were forcing him to wear a mask, a mask that said, "I'm not so bad because I'm doing better than 50 percent of kids like me." It frustrated me because it threatened the very thing that I love about Lucas. He is real, incapable of pretending, and he never wears masks. He is who he is. He is who God created him to be.

Lucas has taught me to throw out my collection of masks and to be real. He has taught me to focus on improving my personal best and challenged me to strive for the approval of the One who created me rather than spending my time and energy seeking the approval of men.

In 1 Thessalonians 2:4-6, Paul writes, "We are not trying to please men but God, who tests our hearts. You know we never used flattery, nor did we put on a mask to cover up greed—God is our witness. We were not looking for praise from men." Paul wasn't interested in wearing a mask to improve his reputation or to gain the praises of people. He simply wanted to please God.

When our oldest son, Hans, was a junior in high school, I took him to a men's conference in Des Moines, which happened to take place in the same arena as the annual state basketball tournaments. As we left the event Friday night, he expressed how much he would love to return to that arena to play a tournament game with his team. Hans is a very good ball player. People love to watch him. He is often highlighted on the sports page for his exceptional offensive performance and was the only junior to be elected first-team, all-conference in 2005.

With this type of success, I knew it would be natural for Hans to focus on the glory and begin playing for the cheers of the crowd. His comments provided me the perfect opportunity to discuss the importance of seeking God's approval above all else. I simply said, "Hans, I don't care how many people show up to watch you play, or how many cameras are on you, stay narrowly focused on playing for an audience of One. Play for God's approval, not the approval of your coach. Play for God's pleasure, not your mom's and mine. Play for God, not your peers. He is the One that gave you the talent and resolve to play the game with excellence. Play it for Him."

The movie *Chariots of Fire* tells the true story of Olympic runner Eric Liddell. When sharing his passion for running, Liddell says, "I believe that God made me for a purpose, but he also made me fast, and when I run, I feel God's pleasure." He recognized the source of his talent and he understood the concept of playing for an audience of One.[3]

When Duke basketball guard J.J. Redick was interviewed about his near-perfect free-throw record, he described his technique step-by-step: Step to the line, square-up the body, see the hoop, dribble once, spin the ball, dribble once more, spin the ball, recite Philippians 4:13, "I can do all things through Christ who gives me strength," and shoot.[4] What a testimony of authenticity. Redick wasn't afraid to remove the mask of stud athlete and admit, on national television, that he depends on God for his strength.

Trying to please people can make your life incredibly complicated. Everyone you come into contact with has a different standard of success and a different opinion of how to achieve it. But living only for God's pleasure simplifies your life and gives you the freedom to take risks. He already knows your deficiencies, yet He loves you as though you are perfect. His opinion of you is not formed according to your power, prestige, or possessions, so you can take risks without the fear of rejection.

When I left Sheldon High School to work at Opportunities Unlimited, my dad, who is generally supportive of my life decisions, thought I was crazy. The first time I told Darla I wanted to run for governor, she had three words for me, and they weren't, "I love you." They were, "Are you nuts?" In fact, there were many who questioned that decision and told me I simply couldn't, and shouldn't, do it. But I was, and remain, determined to play for an audience of One.

When you feel a particular call placed on your heart, and you are sincere about solely pleasing the Lord, then you leave a job that makes sense and a position that is respected, and you take a leap of faith. You risk your reputation, and you campaign for a political office that most people say is nearly impossible to attain. Even if the outcome seems like a failure in the eyes of the world, I have achieved success if I have truly acted in obedience, seeking to please the Lord.

Too often, the fear of failure holds us captive. We don't want to look foolish, so we don't take risks that we believe God wants us to take. But His kingdom is far more important than what other people think of us, and true success is not about living up to the world's standards. True success is about knowing the living God. When you understand your identity as a child of the King, your politically correct reputation becomes far less significant and you are able to boldly pursue His pleasure.

How do you please Him? You throw away your masks and you risk being real. You risk looking foolish. You develop a new measure of success, realizing that the one within you is far more important than those around you. And you begin to play for an audience of One—playing hard in spite of obstacles, playing hard in spite of popular opinion, and never underestimating the Spirit of God. He is the one who gives you the strength to be authentic, to put aside cheap imitations and be the person He created you to be.

♦ ♦   ♦ ♦   ♦ ♦   ♦ ♦   ♦ ♦   ♦ ♦   ♦ ♦   ♦ ♦   ♦ ♦   ♦ ♦

Dear Lucas,

Do you ever wonder or care what people think about you? I know, dumb question. I can tell by your actions that you really don't care.

Throwing your cup after drinking its contents doesn't "fly" in most social circles. Sharing your chosen emotion with a multi-pitched scream is quite the attention-getter in any setting. Closing your eyes and pretending to sleep while someone is trying desperately to entertain you has an imme-

diate and humbling effect. And my personal favorite, laughing uncontrollably while filling your pants, takes the meaning of "manhood" to a whole new level.

Mom is quick to tell me not to encourage these behaviors. I agree you have areas that may need some brushing up, but I must admit that I love your authenticity. It's a breath of fresh air (save the filling the pants while laughing stunt) in a stuffy society where people take themselves, their dress, their position, and their words way too seriously.

You are you all the time. When you're happy, people know you're happy. When you're mad or sad, they know you're mad or sad. When you're grumpy and tired, your emotions say you are grumpy and tired. When you're excited to see us, or listen to a song, or go for a ride, every stitch of your demeanor says you're excited. You don't harbor or display any false emotions. You are Lucas: crystal clear, 100 percent authentic—all the time.

My world encourages the use of masks and the art of spin. You have taught me to be real. Believe me, I'm not as real as you are, but I'm gaining. I'm learning to take myself and my inadequacies less seriously and I love you for that.

I love you for who you are. Lucas, you are beautiful all the time. You were knit together in Mom's womb by our Father in heaven, and every one of your days was ordained for you before you were even born. There is only one you, and you never try to hide who you really are by wearing a socially acceptable mask.

Thank you for simply being you. I love you, kid!
Dad

Chapter Five

You Are Never Alone

For 11 years I was surrounded by high school students, teachers, and parents. I loved it. For me, the greatest reward of serving as an educator, whether in the classroom or as a principal, was experiencing people. Young or old, people inspire me.

Following my career in education I became a public speaker, leading teacher in-services, student assemblies, and business seminars, and working with various corporate boards. These are opportunities that I still have today. I love it. It is inspiring when you have the opportunity to touch people's lives, if only for a moment.

When I entered the political world as a candidate for governor, I spent hundreds of hours visiting communities across Iowa, meeting with citizens and leaders. I loved it. It was great fun experiencing different cultures within the same state, talking with people about their concerns, and participating in their celebrations—networking, networking, networking to build my team.

My entire adult life has been about people. I have chosen careers and volunteer efforts that have kept me surrounded by people of all ages, social and economic backgrounds, and political positions. I love being with people.

There have been times in my life, though, when I have been with literally hundreds of people yet I've felt drastically alone. It is truly a paradox.

I have come to realize that my feelings of loneliness have had much less to do with the number of people around me and much more to do with who is controlling my life. You've surely heard the saying, "There's strength in numbers." True. You've heard it said, "Many hands make light work." True again. But, you've also heard, "Too many cooks spoil the broth." The very best plans will turn to chaos unless there is someone leading—a leader who is skilled at blending individual talents to fulfill a compelling vision.

We human beings love to be in control, spending excessive amounts of time and energy on things that benefit our own desires. "Don't give me the copilot seat. I'll fly this plane!" I like "piloting" my own life because it feels good to be in control. If you are honest with yourself, you probably like it too. We enjoy controlling our own agenda as long as everything is going smoothly.

Flying without a pilot's license, however, can be fatal.

When on the campaign trail, I had many opportunities to fill the copilot's chair of private aircraft and observe the intricacies of flying. The instrument panel is like a living object, with various gauges constantly moving and changing. Through the headsets come frequent air tower communications that may or may not be intended for your aircraft. And then there are the manuals and maps throughout the cockpit.

As much as I would love to fly the plane, and as often as I've been the passenger, putting me in the pilot seat would surely end in disaster. If I want to get to my destination alive, I need to have a pilot who understands where we came from, where we're going, and how to get there. Just as a successful flight requires a skilled pilot, a successful life requires a God who understands where we came from, where we need to go, and how to get us there. It requires us to surrender control and submit to His agenda, putting our own ambitions aside. We must let God be our pilot.

When I insist on taking the pilot seat, I find myself exhausted and stressed, attempting to do what I am not qualified to do. But moving to my rightful place as copilot removes the pressure. It puts God in charge, and knowing that I'm not alone returns the bounce to my step.

Even so, there are times when I grasp for control with all my might, fiercely determined to fly my plane. It is at these times, fighting a losing battle for control, when I feel desperately alone. Countless times when Lucas has hung in the balance between life and death, I've been left feeling powerless and alone.

One evening Darla was working in the kitchen and holding Lucas, while Hans, Josh, and I visited at the kitchen table. When Darla reached to retrieve a glass from the cupboard, she heard Lucas take in a long, deep breath. She expected, of course, to hear it followed by an equal exhale but one never came. She recalls looking down at him lying in her arms and realizing that he had stopped breathing. Immediately, she called to me for help. I scooped him up and ran to the living room. Darla was right behind me. When I put Lucas on the floor to begin rescue breathing, Darla knelt down beside us, close to hysteria. Hans and Josh, a kindergartener and a preschooler, looked on as their brother's life was slipping away right in front of their eyes.

Grabbing the phone, I told Hans to dial 9-1-1. I remember tilting Lucas's head back, putting my mouth over his, and reciting the steps in my mind that I had learned in CPR training. I never thought I'd have to use that training, especially on my own son, but it would be the first of many times. At that moment, clutching his tiny body and breathing into his mouth, I felt powerless. No matter the method I used or how well I performed it, I was incapable of making him respond.

I remember Darla regaining her composure. I remember telling Hans and Josh to run to the front yard and watch for the ambulance. They needed to leave the room because I didn't want them to see their little brother die on the living room floor. I was relying solely on CPR training and human efforts for security, yet feeling completely powerless and alone.

In August of 1995, when Lucas was two years old, Darla and I attended the Lissencephaly Network conference in Boston to expand our knowledge of Lucas's condition and build a network of support. We took all three boys, and since they would outnumber us, we beefed up the troops by bringing a caregiver along.

The doctor had given us a prescription for Lucas; it was supposed to help him better handle the flight to Boston. Though the flight went okay, we became aware throughout the day that something wasn't quite right. After arriving in Boston, we brought Lucas to the emergency room.

As you know by now, we were very familiar with emergency room visits. The medical staff members at this particular hospital, however, were not familiar with Lucas. They tried relentlessly to establish an IV line, eventually getting it done. But it wasn't long before the line blew, and they had to repeat the whole painful process. It was painful for Lucas to experience and painful for us to watch. He absolutely looked like a pincushion. Darla pleaded with the medical staff to insert the line in his neck where his veins are much more visible, but they refused.

They observed Lucas for a couple of days and once he was released, we took him to the conference with us. By lunchtime he had become completely lethargic, not eating or drinking, and we were concerned. The fun family trip and wonderful learning experience that we had anticipated was turning into a series of worries and disappointments.

Reluctantly, but without another option, we returned to the emergency room. This time Darla insisted that they leave Lucas's arms and legs alone. She was so insistent, in fact, that the doctor asked us to leave the room while the medical team tried to establish a line in his neck. Because it was a teaching hospital, there were several interns tending to him, and mistakes were being made that could have been avoided. It was exasperating to watch and our frustration was obvious to the attending physician—so obvious that he didn't want us in the room.

We were overwhelmed with emotion. We had watched our son suffer as he endured a painful, repetitive procedure that seemed futile to us, while all along we had the knowledge and instinct to remedy the situation. We were helpless, full of frustration and anger. As we left the emergency room and entered the elevator, Darla looked at me and said the words that captured my sentiment as well, "There is no God."

We felt so alone. If there was a God, why would He put Lucas through that? Lucas hadn't done anything wrong and he didn't deserve any of it. He wasn't obnoxious, defiant, or naughty. He was incapable of willful sins. If there was a God, surely He would have rescued Lucas from all the ugliness. Surely He would have taken him home to heaven where his suffering would be over. Surely He could have healed our son so he wouldn't have had to endure the pain.

We stood silent in the elevator. When the doors opened, Darla went one way and I went the other. We needed time apart. The ironic thing is that we each used the time apart to pray to the God whose existence we had just denied.

After a while we returned to the elevator. In the midst of an emotional embrace, we both confessed that there was indeed a God and that He was the only one with the strength to get us, and Lucas, through these painful times. When we admitted that we were powerless and surrendered control, He carried us through.

When Lucas was six years old, Darla and I reached the very difficult decision to seek full-time care for him. We were struggling to adequately meet his needs at home while still caring for his three brothers, so we admitted him to Children's Care Hospital and School in Sioux Falls, South Dakota.

You've heard of empty-nest syndrome. So had we. But the sorrow and anxiety a parent experiences when an adult child goes to college or gets married doesn't compare to the discomfort of leaving a six-year-old in the hands of others and walking away knowing that he is alone.

The most frustrating emotion Darla and I experienced during those first few days was that of guilt. It was not the guilt of leaving Lucas but the guilt of feeling relieved. We felt so good about the decision, knowing that it was a wonderful facility and that he would be well cared for according to his unique needs.

Returning home to Sioux City, we experienced a full night of sleep. Before that, we'd had an arrangement where Darla would get up in the night with the baby, Logan, because her body was better equipped to meet his demands. And I would get up with Lucas. Whether summoned by cries or monitor alarms, when Lucas had a need in the night, I would get up to be with him. Many mornings, he would wake up very early. In an effort to keep the rest of the family from being disturbed, I would put Lucas into one of our vehicles, and we would take a morning cruise (something he still loves to this day).

The decrease in demands after moving Lucas to CCHS was refreshing, but there were also times during the separation process when we felt desperately alone, questioning our decision. We were depending on other people to raise the son that God entrusted to us, and that was a difficult reality at times. Even now, years later, we experience moments of guilt as we kiss Lucas good-bye and make the drive back to Sioux City, but we believe wholeheartedly we are doing what is best for him. And we know that God is with him. Deuteronomy 31:8 promises that "the LORD himself goes before you and will be with you; he will never leave you nor forsake you."

Despite the many difficult decisions and emergency situations we have had with Lucas, our loneliest moments came in the spring of 2004 when he was scheduled for full spinal fusion surgery at the University of Iowa Hospital. The doctor explained that it would be a long surgery—about six hours—and that Lucas would lose nearly 60 percent of his blood. The discs in his back would be removed, allowing the spine to collapse, then the surgeons would strategically place rods along the spine until it was straightened. A mere cold can send Lucas into seizures, resulting in life or death situations, so we knew this surgery was going to be a major event. And we felt very alone.

On Wednesday, April 6, Darla and I took Lucas to Iowa City for his surgery. After checking into our hotel room, the three of us lay on the bed together as I read from Psalm 139:

O LORD, you have searched me and you know me. You know when I sit and when I rise; you perceive my thoughts from afar. You discern my going out and my lying down; you are familiar with all my ways. Before a word is on my tongue you know it completely. . . . Where can I go from your Spirit? Where can I flee from your presence? If I go up to the heavens, you are there; if I make my bed in the depths, you are there. If I rise on the wings of the dawn, if I settle on the far side of the sea, even there your hand will guide me, your right hand will hold me fast.

If I say, "Surely the darkness will hide me and the light

become night around me," even the darkness will not be dark
to you; the night will shine like the day, for darkness is as light
to you.

For you created my inmost being; you knit me together in
my mother's womb. I praise you because I am fearfully and
wonderfully made; your works are wonderful, I know that full
well. My frame was not hidden from you when I was made
in the secret place. When I was woven together in the depths
of the earth, your eyes saw my unformed body. All the days
ordained for me were written in your book before one of them
came to be.

We understood the severity of Lucas's surgery and knew that
these could be his last days. Because I believe the only way to
heaven is through Christ's sacrifice, my heart was burdened for
Lucas's salvation.

After reading Psalm 139, we prayed. We thanked God that we
can't ever flee from His presence and that He knows the number
of our days. We thanked God for the gift of Lucas. We prayed that
God would hold Lucas in His arms through the surgery. And we
prayed a very personal prayer on behalf of Lucas, receiving Christ's
gift of eternal life. Although Lucas couldn't nod in agreement or
say the words, we know that God answered that prayer. Those intimate moments gave Darla and me great comfort as we sent Lucas
into surgery.

The surgery went as expected, but Lucas battled to recover for
two months. Many of his days were spent in the intensive care
unit. Many were spent in, or near, critical condition. We were
required to make numerous difficult decisions during those
months and saw his temperature reach 107 degrees. It was a day-
to-day struggle with many fearful moments.

At one point Lucas was even taken back into surgery. The doctors needed to irrigate his incision because he had developed a staph infection. With a sky-high fever and extended periods of unconsciousness, we thought we were going to lose him. Darla and I prayed for God's will to be done, but we also prayed that if it was his time, God would take Lucas quickly, while he was at peace under the anesthetic.

As we sat in the surgical waiting room, Darla and I began planning a funeral for our son. In a strange way, I hoped that God would take him home. He deserved to be whole and happy. He deserved to see Christ's face and to feel the embrace of a Savior who also endured suffering through no guilt of His own. I just wanted Lucas's suffering to be over. Spending time in prayer truly brought us peace. In fact, after planning and praying, Darla wrapped herself up in Lucas's Scooby-Doo blanket and put her head on my shoulder. I rested my head on hers and we both fell asleep.

Every time I've tried to be my own pilot, trying to make sense of chaos and control circumstances, I am left feeling fatigued and alone. But every time I've stayed purposely in my copilot seat, turning my focus to prayer and the truth in God's Word, I've found peace. Every time. Surrendering control and submitting to God's perfect will floods my soul with comfort and replaces feelings of loneliness with a powerful awareness that I am never alone. He never leaves. Even when I try to escape His presence, He's there.

I sometimes wear a silver chain that has a shield hanging from it. On the back of the shield, these words are engraved: "Be strong and courageous. Do not be terrified; do not be discouraged, for the LORD your God will be with you wherever you go" (Joshua 1:9). Psalm 139, the one we read to Lucas before his surgery, assures us that we cannot flee from God's presence. If you go up to the heavens, He is there. If you make your bed in the depths, He is there.

If you go into a surgical room without your mom and dad, He is there. If you live at a full-time care facility away from your family, He is there. If you stand in your living room watching your son's life slipping away, He is there. If you see your child suffering, crying out in pain, He is there.

What situations are you dealing with today that have made you feel powerless and alone? Get out of the pilot seat, cease your efforts for control, and allow God to navigate your life. He is there for you and He longs to see the bounce return to your step and the sparkle to your eye.

I still love to be surrounded by people. That hasn't changed. But I've learned that speaking at big events and leading teams of executives in boardroom discussions cannot be the source of my security. Lucas, a kid who lives a life of solitude, has taught me that security is found simply in knowing that we are never alone. He has taught me the precious truth that when life brings situations beyond our control and heartache beyond reason, God is always there to see us through.

♦ ♦   ♦ ♦   ♦ ♦   ♦ ♦   ♦ ♦   ♦ ♦   ♦ ♦   ♦ ♦   ♦ ♦   ♦ ♦

Dear Lucas,

Every time you go "code blue," Mom and I, along with anyone else in the room, go "code scared-to-death." I'm sure you see the fear in our eyes and hear the fear in our voices. I'm sure our fear does nothing to comfort you as you struggle to hold on to life, and I'm sorry for that.

I know you feel alone and frightened each time you enter a seizure or an unstable medical condition. I see the fear in your eyes too. I wish so much that I could say just the right words or do just the right thing to take your fear away. But, if I were you, I would be scared too.

God tells us in His Word to "be strong and courageous. Do not be terrified; do not be discouraged" (Joshua 1:9). Your fight for life has proven over and over again that God's instruction is easier said than done. When you stop breathing, you're scared. When you hear an ambulance coming and you know it's coming for you, you're scared. When you see needles being prepared . . . you're scared.

The reason God tells you, "Do not be afraid," is because He is with you—always. He will never leave you, Lucas. I wish I could tell you that God will never let you hurt again, but I can't. The only promise I can make is that He loves you, He loves your mom and me, and He will never let us face life's struggles alone.

Even though I have run both to and from God during your medical emergencies, He has never moved. Every time I have been filled with fear, afraid of losing you, God's love and embrace have been evident.

If we could, Mom and I would be with you constantly, but we simply can't. So my fervent prayer for you is that you will feel the power of God's love and embrace all the time, every minute of every day.

Never forget, Lucas, that you will never be alone. God's love, Mom's love, and my love are with you always.

Dad

Chapter Six

Thank You, God, for Moms

Darla and I had our first date on Friday, December 12, 1980. She is still impressed that I recall the exact date, since men don't have the best track record of remembering such details, but my reason is very simple. I remember it in detail because it was the day I found the perfect woman—at least the perfect woman for me.

We were both seniors in high school and she was beautiful. Our high school basketball team had a game that night, and she was going to the game to watch me play. When I picked her up that evening, she hoarsely explained that she had a case of laryngitis. I remember thinking, *Life doesn't get much better than this: a beautiful girl—who can't talk—is accompanying me to my basketball game.* It was perfect.

Darla and I were very different from one another. She was a great student. She loved to read. She studied hard. She was on the honor roll. When her parents needed to issue her a punishment, they restricted her reading time. Now, if my parents would have used the same method of punishment, I would have been all for it. Sign me up, Mom and Dad. When I mess up, don't let me read for two or three days, or better yet, two or three months!

Darla was awarded academic scholarships, music scholarships, and presidential scholarships, and she graduated summa cum laude from Northwestern College. Darla and I shared the last name Vander Plaats by the time of our college graduation. (We had been married for nearly two years.) So when they announced the graduates in alphabetical order, the D in Darla came before the R in Robert. They announced Darla's name, followed by the title of summa cum laude, and I remember thinking, "What did they just call her?" Of course, when they announced my name, it was simply Robert L. Vander Plaats. End of introduction.

Darla was focused on developing her career. She was going to take the accounting profession by storm, passing the entire CPA exam on her first try. Again, I saw her as the perfect woman: smart, beautiful, great earning potential, yet she always allowed me to believe that I was the leader of our home. She was supportive of my career as a teacher and coach, knowing that she would be the primary breadwinner.

But an amazing transition took place on February 23, 1988, with the birth of our first child, Hans. All of a sudden we were both experiencing the emotions of parenthood. Darla took a long sabbatical from her career and, when the time came to return, she struggled in her search to find a caregiver for Hans. Once she selected someone, it was incredibly difficult for Darla to put our baby in someone else's arms each morning on her way to the office. Her priorities had shifted dramatically, and her career was no longer her primary focus. What mattered more was being a mom.

Three years later along came our second son, Josh. Up to that point Darla remained engaged as a CPA with an accounting firm, and I was still teaching and coaching while pursuing my master's degree and running a landscaping business. With the birth of Josh, Darla was convinced it was time to leave her career and focus on raising our sons. It was a difficult decision, but we both believe that moms and dads should be the primary caregivers whenever possible. Trusting God to provide for our financial needs, we made the decision for Darla to become a stay-at-home mom.

Soon after making that decision I accepted an offer to become a high school principal. The position came with a larger salary and better benefits, making it easier for Darla to stay at home. Though it was an adjustment, we settled into the idea that Darla would be a full-time mom and I would be the primary breadwinner. It was a much different life than we had envisioned back in college, but I believe it was God's way of preparing us for the birth of Lucas.

He knew that Lucas would require focused attention. If Lucas had been born into a different situation, he may not have survived. But the love, care, and abundant time that Darla has been able to provide is likely the reason he has progressed to where he is today.

Stepping away from her career didn't rob Darla of her intelligence or squelch her ability to learn things quickly. In fact, she employed her love of learning to study Lucas's diagnosis, procedures, and medications. She has become articulate with the medical community, able to communicate with doctors and nurses regarding Lucas's needs. I have seen her remain poised, offering lifesaving information in the midst of emergency situations.

When the medical community has been willing to work with us, particularly Darla, Lucas has been spared unnecessary and painful procedures. His quality of care has been enhanced through Darla's input, and not only through her knowledge of the facts, but through her instinct, her mother's intuition.

When Lucas was recovering from full spinal fusion surgery, I became acutely aware of the difference between doctors and moms. Lucas had been on a ventilator following surgery and when they removed the breathing tube, he went into severe distress. The room filled immediately with medical professionals employing their best efforts to stabilize him, but he was unresponsive. Then Darla made a suggestion that would ultimately save our son's life. She watched nervously as the professionals worked on him without result, then said, "Let's give him a bolus of Ativan so that we will know if his issue is seizure related or if it's something else." Without hesitation, without committees, and without questions the doctor in charge followed Darla's advice, and Lucas responded exactly as she predicted. As the doctor left the intensive care room that day, he looked at my dad and said, "Thank God for moms."

Doctors are intensely educated individuals with high IQs and thousands of hours of experience. They stay up-to-date on research and use proven methods to save lives every day. They deserve our respect and our thanks.

Moms, on the other hand, may not have medical degrees or teaching certificates. They may not appear wise according to the world's standards, but they have an uncanny awareness of what their children need. In 1 Corinthians 1:27 we read, "God chose the foolish things of the world to shame the wise . . . the weak things of the world to shame the strong." This passage reminds us to value instinct over intellect, making a lifesaving judgment call without opening a textbook, for instance, and saying or doing exactly what needs to be said or done, void of degrees or certificates.

Lucas is incredibly blessed to have a mom who absorbs knowledge quickly and is tireless in pursuing information about his condition, advocating for him in a way that is respected by the medical community. But more important is Darla's keen awareness of what is best for him simply because she's his mom.

A most popular Scripture passage for Mother's Day sermons is chapter 31 of Proverbs. It's great material for a touching lesson, but even more powerful has been the opportunity to see those verses demonstrated through Darla's life.

Proverbs 31:11-12 says, "Her husband has full confidence in her and lacks nothing of value. She brings him good, not harm. . . ." Darla embodies these verses, always giving me her full support in major life decisions. And her support has made me appreciate her character. She supported my career as a teacher and coach and was excited when I had the opportunity to become a high school principal. While in the midst of raising three young children, one with severe disabilities, she supported my decision to leave the security of the public school system and become the president and CEO of an ailing nonprofit organization. She even supported my campaign for governor, despite the overwhelming odds and my extensive travel schedule.

Proverbs 31 also celebrates a woman's hard work and the care she gives to her family: "She sets about her work vigorously. . . . She watches over the affairs of her household and does not eat the bread of idleness" (verses 17, 27). Again, I see this in Darla. I am inspired by the selfless attention she devotes to our family. Not only does she give specialized care to Lucas, but she also invests an incredible amount of time and energy into the lives of Hans, Josh, and Logan. When on the campaign trail, Darla was asked about her potential agenda as the state's First Lady. She confidently answered, "If I'm provided the opportunity to be your First Lady, my first role will be as First Mom." It made me wish for a greater number of politically involved parents willing to commit first to their families and then to their constituents.

Proverbs 31:20 talks about service, and Darla loves to serve. She possesses many talents yet has a beautiful spirit of humility.

She serves our church with her musical gift by playing the piano and organ. She serves young moms in the Mothers of Preschoolers program. She serves the boys' schools, working in elementary classrooms and facilitating high school fundraisers. If she knows of an unmet need, she seeks to serve. I love that about her, because she's teaching our sons to think of others above themselves.

She is also teaching them about integrity. Proverbs 31:25-26 says, "She is clothed with strength and dignity. . . . She speaks with wisdom, and faithful instruction is on her tongue." Anyone who knows Darla recognizes her strength of character and the wisdom with which she speaks. She has modeled the character of Christ to our children and to me. In large part, it is Darla's standard of integrity that inspired me to run a positive political campaign. When strategists were advising us to attack, we stayed committed to giving people something to vote for, not something to vote against. Why? Because our boys were watching and they were learning how to relate to the world around them.

Though Darla is a beautiful woman on the outside, her inner beauty has captured my heart. "Charm is deceptive, and beauty is fleeting; but a woman who fears the LORD is to be praised" (Proverbs 31:30). Darla seeks the Lord with passion. He is her first love, and that is what makes her truly beautiful.

Finally, Proverbs 31 recognizes the praise due to a woman of noble character: "Her children arise and call her blessed; her husband also, and he praises her" (verse 28). The boys and I are far from perfect in the way we uphold Darla, failing often to give her the honor that she deserves. But we absolutely adore her for the wife, mother, and friend that she is to us and for the inspiration she gives us to be better men.

The Pharisees were the religious men of Jesus' day, well-educated in biblical facts. They knew the law, and were tenacious in promoting it—every *i* dotted, every *t* crossed. The Pharisees focused on matters of the intellect. But Jesus rocked their system by speaking of compassion and forgiveness. He promoted servant-hood and the practice of examining your own actions rather than judging the actions of others. He focused on matters of the heart.

A mother's worth can't be measured academically. Her worth doesn't lie within her intellect, but within the fabric of her soul. It lies in the instinctive decisions that she makes on behalf of her family, not in the knowledge accumulated from textbooks.

Of course our society should sincerely thank the professionals for their expertise. We need to thank teachers for instructing our children in mathematics, the sciences, and the arts. We need to thank doctors and nurses for the countless hours they've spent per-fecting their skills in order to save lives and provide relief from strep throat and diaper rash. We need to appreciate the significance knowledge and technology have in our society. But more than that, we need to celebrate moms, who teach us the stuff of life that isn't contained in the classroom. We need to celebrate their love, care, and beauty. And we need to celebrate the wisdom they impart to their children and on behalf of their children, wisdom that is born within the heart of a mother when she looks upon the face of her son or daughter, knowing she has the privilege and responsi-bility of commissioning the next generation.

Observing Darla's love and care for Lucas has both humbled and inspired me. She will never receive a diploma for her perform-ance as his mother. She'll never hear him say the words "thank you" or "I love you," but she remains passionate in her love for him and diligent in her duty to him. I believe it's a beautiful picture of what God intended moms to be. Not perfect. Not famous. Not even summa cum laude. Just lovers of their children, no matter what. And in the words of Lucas's doctor, thank God for moms!

❦ ❦   ❦ ❦   ❦ ❦   ❦ ❦   ❦ ❦   ❦ ❦   ❦ ❦   ❦ ❦   ❦ ❦   ❦ ❦

Dear Lucas,

You have a special mom. I've known she's a special person for a long time, but your birth allowed me to see her beauty in a new way. She loves you very much.

Your mom went through a lot when she gave birth to you. But in typical style, her concern was not for herself, it was for you. She wanted to make sure that you were in good care. She even convinced the doctors to release her from the hospital early so she could be with you.

I don't believe you would be alive today had you been born to someone besides your mother. She has startled the medical community and the experts with her knowledge and instincts for your care. What makes her care so special is that it is completely motivated by her love for you.

The decision to put you in someone else's care was clearly the toughest decision your mom and I have ever made. It was painful, to say the least. It still pains us to leave for home after our visits with you. And we only find peace because we know it is God's best for you and our family. I hope you understand.

I know you love it when we visit. My greatest pleasure during our times together is watching the bond between you and Mom. You both escape the monotony and struggles of this world when you're together. Mom's embrace, her songs, and her total presence reveal her love for you and her thanks to God. Seeing the way you gaze into Mom's face with such love and contentment is like seeing a masterpiece.

Mom talks often of her desire to be in heaven with you. You better set aside a great deal of time for that heavenly reunion! She wants to experience all that has been missing from this life. She wants to see you walk, hear you sing, and dance the streets of gold with you. What a day that will be! I hope you two won't mind if I join in!

I believe God gives us moms to help us understand the tender love He has for us. Lucas, I hope you thank God every day that He has given you such a beautiful picture of His love.

> *I love you, kid!*
> *Dad*

Chapter Seven

♦ ♦ ♦ ♦ ♦ ♦ ♦ ♦ ♦ ♦ ♦ ♦ ♦ ♦ ♦ ♦ ♦ ♦ ♦ ♦

There Are Angels Among Us

In his book *Echoes of the Maggid,* Rabbi Paysach Krohn tells the story of a man who delivered a speech to the attendees of a fund-raising dinner for his son's school, a school dedicated to serving children with disabilities.

After praising the school's dedicated staff, the father shocked the audience by crying out, "Where is the perfection in my son Shaya? Everything that God does is done with perfection. But my child cannot understand things as other children do. My child cannot remember facts and figures as other children do. Where is God's perfection?" His voice was anguished as he went on to tell the story of how God revealed his son's perfection.

One Sunday afternoon he and his son Shaya went on a walk by the local park where a group of boys were playing a game of baseball. The boy wanted to play. Though Shaya was obviously not athletic, one of the boys agreed to have him join their team, since they were losing by six runs and the game was almost over. The father was ecstatic as he watched his son run onto the field.

By the bottom of the ninth inning, Shaya's team was losing by two runs, had two outs, and the bases were loaded. And it was Shaya's turn to bat. Nervously, the father watched his son awkwardly hold the bat and step up to the plate.

The pitcher stepped toward home plate and gently lobbed the ball to Shaya, who swung clumsily and missed. Trying to help, one of his teammates stepped behind Shaya and prepared to help him swing. Again, the pitcher stepped closer and tossed the ball. This time, Shaya hit the ball and it bounced across the ground to the pitcher. The pitcher picked up the soft grounder and could easily have thrown the ball to the first baseman. Shaya would have been out and that would have ended the game.

Instead, the pitcher took the ball and threw it on a high arc to right field, far and wide beyond the first baseman's reach. Everyone started yelling, "Shaya, run to first! Shaya, run to first!" Never in his life had Shaya run to first.

He scampered down the baseline wide-eyed and startled. The right fielder caught the ball before Shaya reached first base, but Shaya rounded the baseline and kept running. It could have been an easy out at second base. But the right fielder understood what the pitcher's intentions were, so he threw the ball high and far over the third baseman's head, as everyone yelled, "Shaya, run to second! Shaya, run to second!"

Shaya ran to second base as the runners ahead of him deliriously circled the bases toward home. As Shaya reached second base, the opposing shortstop ran toward him, turned him in the direction of third base, and shouted "Shaya, run to third!"

As Shaya rounded third, the boys from both teams ran behind him screaming, "Shaya, run home! Shaya, run home!" Shaya ran home and stepped on home plate, and all 18 boys lifted him on their shoulders and made him the hero, as he had just hit the "grand slam" and won the game for his team.

"That day," said the father who now had tears rolling down his face, "those 18 boys reached their level of perfection."[5]

Every time I hear or relay the story of Shaya and his father, tears roll down my face as well, and emotion fills my voice. It is a rare picture of two teams, 18 boys, sacrificing their desire to win so that Shaya could experience what it felt like to be the hero. That is God's perfection!

Shaya's story has helped me to realize that God has displayed His perfection through Lucas time and time again, not through his disabilities but in how people have responded to his disabilities. You see, God's purpose for Lucas isn't for Lucas. It's for us. God's purpose for you and me isn't for you and me. It's for others. God's purpose for His children is to reveal His glory through the impact we have on others.

When Lucas attended preschool at Clark Elementary in Sioux City, his teacher frequently took him to a third grade classroom so the students could experience community with a child with disabilities. Throughout the school year the kids grew comfortable with Lucas and truly enjoyed having him in their classroom.

In the spring of that year, while watching Josh play a Little League baseball game against some of the students from Clark Elementary, we had the opportunity to see the result of a teacher's effort to show a group of students the importance of community. We were sitting just outside the fence by first base, and Lucas was on a blanket by our feet. We watched the pitch. Crack! The batter hit a line drive to the shortstop, who promptly scooped up the ball and threw it to the first baseman. Unfortunately, the ball flew past the first baseman and hit the fence just in front of us. When the boy playing first base ran to retrieve the ball, he looked over at Lucas, then stopped and said, "Hey Lucas. How you doin'?" By the time he picked up the ball and threw it to second, the runner was safe.

It was a precious reminder that people are more important than baseball. Friends are more important than winning. With a smile and a few kind words, this young first baseman showed that he valued Lucas above his own agenda. Jesus' entire ministry was about putting the cause above self—spreading the truth of God's love, power, and forgiveness even when it compromised His comfort, desires, and even His own life.

Many of my days have been spent teaching leadership strategies and working with business executives to maximize the potential of their organizations. We use words such as *character, integrity, excellence*, and *leadership*. At times these words can seem so vague and so intangible. It's hard to wholly define integrity, but you know it when you see it. It is difficult to adequately describe excellence, but you know it when you see it.

In the same way, the words *Christian community* can be elusive. Churches have become diligent in promoting Christian community, but many times the result is simply another program or committee. Although the concept of Christian community can be vague, you know it when you see it, and we see it in the life of Jesus over and over again. He continually offered a helping hand and kind words to passersby, always compassionate to those with special needs. He took time to see people's hidden hurts and to love the unlovely.

The book of Matthew records several of Jesus' encounters with those in need. Matthew 8:3 describes how He shows compassion to a man with leprosy. We can assume that the man was covered with grotesque sores, yet Jesus "reached out his hand and touched the man" and the man was immediately healed. I wonder how long it had been since he had felt the touch of a friend.

Later the same chapter reveals how Jesus heals Peter's mother-in-law. "He touched her hand and the fever left her, and she got up and began to wait on him" (Matthew 8:15). Again, He showed kindness through touch.

In chapter 9, we read about Jesus healing several people. He heals a paralyzed man and a woman who had been plagued with a bleeding disorder for much of her life. He brings a man's daughter back to life by touching her hand. He touches the eyes of two blind men and restores their sight. He restores speech to a mute man.

Jesus helped people over and over again, meeting their needs through the miraculous power of touch. He was compulsive about showing compassion. Why do you suppose the Scriptures give so much attention to this aspect of our Savior? I don't believe the purpose is to show what a great person He was, but to demonstrate how much He values servanthood. He left us an example to follow, and His example pleads with us to humble ourselves and touch the lives of those in need.

He is the God of the universe. He could have performed mass healings in the blink of an eye, but He chose instead to come face-to-face with hurting people, to physically touch them. He didn't write them a check and send them on their way. He didn't form a committee to look into their situations. He didn't give them a list of expectations or sign them up for a seminar. He found them in the streets, looked them in the eye, put His arm around them, and met their needs.

Paul tells us in Romans 15:4 that everything written in Scripture is written to teach us. Matthew 12:18 and 20 tell us that Jesus was a kind and compassionate servant: "A bruised reed he will not break, and a smoldering wick he will not snuff out." Jesus consistently showed kindness to people with disabilities, and He expects the same from us. He never ignored the crippled or shamed the weak; He honored them. I believe He desires us to embrace the afflicted—those with special needs—allowing His glory and His perfection to be revealed through our love for them.

The story of Ruth and Naomi in the Old Testament further demonstrates the essence of Christian community. Naomi becomes a widow while living away from the country where she was born and raised. Soon after her husband dies, both of Naomi's adult sons die also, leaving her alone with her two daughters-in-law, Orpah and Ruth. Naomi decides to return to her homeland, but instructs her daughters-in-law, whom she loves, to return to their mothers' homes where they might find new husbands. After many tears Orpah departs, but Ruth insists on accompanying her mother-in-law on the rugged and uncertain journey.

In fact, Ruth pledges unswerving devotion and servanthood to Naomi saying, "Don't urge me to leave you or to turn back from you. Where you go I will go, and where you stay I will stay. Your people will be my people and your God my God. Where you die I will die, and there I will be buried. May the LORD deal with me, be it ever so severely, if anything but death separates you and me" (Ruth 1:16-17). Wow, that's a model of community!

The opportunity to return to her family and have a husband was surely tempting and would certainly have provided more security, but Ruth had compassion for her mother-in-law and wanted to serve her. Ruth knew that Naomi was all alone, and she wanted to care for her. She didn't give money or advice. She gave herself.

Lucas's birth was an instant call for Christian community. We greatly appreciated the phone calls, cards, and casseroles, but we were in desperate need of someone to look us in the face, put caring arms around us, and walk through the pains and needs of our days. And God sent us Ruth. Not the Ruth of the Old Testament, but our Ruth—Ruth Klein.

Soon after Lucas was born, I accepted a high school principal position. Ruth had been the secretary to the Sheldon High School principal for several years, so when I arrived she became my assistant. Ruth readily embraced me as the new principal, and she readily embraced Darla and our boys.

Not only was she accepting of us, but she began to model Christian community to us in a way that we had never experienced before. It was more than saying, "I'm praying for you," though we knew she was. It was more than sending a plate of cookies home to the boys, though she did.

She modeled Christian community when she sat at the hospital with us, just in case we needed something. She demonstrated community by listening to our fears and frustrations and not judging us for them. She would arrive on our doorstep in the middle of the night to watch Hans and Josh, so we could be in the emergency room with Lucas. She held Lucas in her arms when we were exhausted. She rejoiced with us over good news and wept with us when we cried out, "why?"

Ruth's model of Christian community was, and continues to be, her willingness to give herself to us—to literally touch our lives.

She has made personal sacrifices in order to serve our family. When Darla and I moved to Sioux City with the boys, after I became the CEO of Opportunities Unlimited, Ruth was right there with us. She left her home in Sheldon and moved to Sioux City because she believed God wanted her to continue serving our family. She served on the staff of OU as my assistant and, as the years have passed, Ruth has assisted us in our gubernatorial campaigns and with MVP Leadership.

We have been blessed immeasurably by Ruth. She loves our family and has always been there when we've needed her, but she has never asked for anything in return. She hasn't done it for praise; she's never expected to receive a material reward. I believe her biggest reward has been the love she has received in return. She is blessed by the love she receives from Hans, Josh, Lucas, and Logan. She is blessed by the love she receives from Darla and me. I would agree with Shaya's dad, God's perfection is not found in

Lucas's disabilities but in the responses to Lucas's disabilities. His perfection has been displayed through people like Ruth.

I wrote a poem on Lucas's behalf to give Ruth one Christmas. Nestled in a collage of photos—snapshots of Ruth and Lucas together—were these words:

> Ruth is my special friend; I see her quite a bit,
> We do many things together, but sometimes we just clap and sit.
> Ruth says that I am special; I believe her words are true,
> My purposes in life may be many, but one is to impact you.
> Ruth makes me smile and brings my life great joy,
> She sees my inner beauty and says that I'm God's special boy.
> Ruth is a part of my family, just like my parents and brothers,
> What makes Ruth so special is the love that she gives to others.
> When I'm with Ruth, there's a smile on my face,
> She gives special feeling that cannot be replaced.
> Ruth is like an angel; her kindness makes her shine,
> One day she may be your friend, I know she'll always be mine!

Though Lucas cannot talk, I believe these words express his feelings for Ruth.

We need to *be* Christian community. We need to reach out and touch people's lives: meet them where they are; look into their eyes; put our arms around their shoulders; and walk through their pains with them—whatever it takes. *Put cause above self;* this is the life Christ modeled.

Walking this journey with Lucas has taught me that God calls us to follow His example of servanthood and have compassion for the weak and unlovely. We are so thankful for the "angels" God sends our way, to serve us and show us compassion. Ruth has been our angel. She has modeled the spirit of Jesus to us through her hands, her words, her time, her emotion, her commitment, and her love. Experiencing her love and kindness inspires me to be more like Christ.

In His infinite wisdom, God teaches the strong through the weak. It isn't hearing about Shaya's great hit that brings tears to our eyes. It is the mental picture we conjure up: 18 healthy, normal boys with torn jeans and grass-stained knees, throwing off their baseball gloves, emptying the dugout, and jumping up and down. It is picturing the excitement on their dirty faces as they cheer for Shaya to run to the next base. It is the image of a father with tears streaming down his face in joy for his son. And it is the image of a clumsy, disabled boy running to home plate, playing the part of a hero. Our hearts are touched because the story forces us to humble ourselves and seek to be an angel to someone else.

♪ ♪ ♪ ♪ ♪ ♪ ♪ ♪ ♪ ♪ ♪ ♪ ♪ ♪ ♪ ♪ ♪ ♪ ♪ ♪

A LETTER TO LUCAS, FROM RUTH

Dear Lucas,

At some point in our lives we feel that we can change the world. Before you entered my life, I was content with my circumstances and the contributions I was making. The Lord had blessed me with a very supportive family. I was active in my church. I loved my job at the local high school where I had the opportunity to work with my best friends every day. We were "impacting the lives" of our students.

Then your dad took the position of high school principal and in only a matter of days I met your mom, your brothers . . . and you. It wasn't long before your mom asked me to ride along on the first of many trips to Sioux Falls for your doctor visits, during which we also stopped at the mall to do some serious shopping!

After that first trip, your mom and I were visiting in the living room when you rolled across the floor to my feet, looked up, and gave me the biggest grin I'd ever seen. From that moment on, Lucas, you've had my heart. And what made it beautiful is that you had no idea. You had nothing to gain and no ulterior motive. You were just being you! It didn't take me long to realize that you were giving me far more than I ever gave to you.

Lucas, you've taught me that it takes no words at all to love someone unconditionally. Spending time with you makes time stand still, with no worries, no pretense, no need to hurry on to something else—just you and me enjoying each other's company.

You've taught me the "little" lessons, like how much happier you are when I walk beside you to guide your chair down the hallway, rather than pushing you from behind. That's what we all want!

Lucas, I've never seen someone's eyes shine quite like yours do when you're excited. And it's your excitement for the simple pleasures that has taught me to actively appreciate the simple pleasures in my own life. You've taught me to fully focus on people I'm spending time with and to tell them how much they mean to me. You've taught me to use more of my time helping and encouraging others, focusing on their unspoken needs.

My life is more beautiful today and it's all because you have changed my world!

Thank you, Lucas! I love you!
Ruth

Chapter Eight

Life Can Tear You Apart or Bond You Together

I was 36 years old when I was invited to share my thoughts about serving people with disabilities at a forum in Washington, D.C. It was to be my first trip to D.C., so I gladly accepted the invitation. In fact, since Darla, Hans, and Josh hadn't been there either, I brought them along so our family could experience our nation's capital together.

Almost immediately upon landing in Washington, D.C. we were confronted with monuments honoring the men and women who have shaped our country's history. The faces and figures of our country's heroes are scattered abundantly throughout D.C., carved in granite and stone. They've been marbleized and memorialized.

Our family spent hours visiting such sites. We viewed the tribute to Thomas Jefferson. We viewed the tributes to Christopher Columbus, George Washington, and Abraham Lincoln. We read about their lives and the sacrifices each one made. Everywhere we went stood these reminders of heroism.

Heroes inspire us. If they didn't, we would not go to such great lengths to honor them with extravagant monuments and immortalize them in books and movies. So what is the essence of a true hero? A hero is a common person who faces extraordinary challenges with uncommon courage, exceptional attitude, and unyielding dignity. A hero is a person who has chosen to rise above circumstance. When others throw their hands up in defeat, the hero presses on and stays the course.

I love to visit Washington, D.C. and celebrate our country's heroes. My soul stirs when I am confronted with the men and women who have gone before me, who have paved the way for my freedoms through intense focus and narrow purpose.

People will always be in search of heroes. More than at any other time in our nation's history, our society seems to be in search of a specific sort of hero—heroes called moms and dads. They may not be aware of it, but today's kids are longing for moms and dads to be champions of marriage, wholly committed to one another for a lifetime. They want to know that their parents are serious about the vows they took, not because the words were pretty but because they gave their word.

The lighting of the unity candle is a beautiful picture of God's plan for marriage. Two individual flames join to make a single flicker of light, an inseparable union symbolizing what God calls "one flesh." Marriage was designed to be between one man and one woman, living as a single entity under the headship of Christ. Regrettably, today's society has come to see marriage as nothing more than a casual agreement. Marriage is no longer defined by oneness, but viewed as a crapshoot with 50/50 odds. Our communities are brimming with failed marriages, broken wedding vows, and moms and dads who have not stayed narrowly focused on their roles as husbands and wives.

Divorce has a sobering effect on children. The Heritage Foundation, a public policy research organization based in Washington, D.C., gave the following report:

Mounting evidence in social science journals demonstrates that the devastating physical, emotional, and financial effects that divorce is having on these children will last well into adulthood and affect future generations. Among these broad and damaging effects are the following:

- Children whose parents have divorced are increasingly the victims of abuse. They exhibit more health, behavioral, and emotional problems, are involved more frequently in crime and drug abuse, and have higher rates of suicide.

- Children of divorced parents perform more poorly in reading, spelling, and math. They also are more likely to repeat a grade and to have higher dropout rates and lower rates of college graduation.

- Families with children that were not poor before the divorce see their income drop as much as 50 percent. Almost 50 percent of the parents with children that are going through a divorce move into poverty after the divorce.

- Religious worship, which has been linked to better health, longer marriages, and better family life, drops after the parents divorce.[6]

The divorce of parents, even if it is amicable, tears apart the fundamental unit of American society. According to the Federal Reserve Board's 1995 Survey of Consumer Finance, only 42 percent of children age 14 to 18 live in a "first marriage" family—an intact, two-parent, married family. It should be no surprise to find that divorce is having such profound effects on society.

On the other hand, children whose biological parents remain

married are more likely to graduate from college, less likely to commit crimes, and statistically healthier physically and emotionally. Any society is stronger when men and women uphold their commitment to marriage. The economy is stronger. The education system is stronger and people of all ages live by a higher standard of morality.

Because of the world we live in, God's perfect plan isn't always realized and divorce happens. When it does, we must pray for God's grace and protection, knowing that "he heals the broken-hearted and binds up their wounds" (Psalm 147:3). I believe that God is deeply saddened by divorce, but He loves His children and His mercies are new every morning.

Marriage is a fundamental pivot point. Civilizations, past and present, are defined by their regard for marriage. And regard for marriage is defined one household at a time.

Darla and I had a picture-perfect beginning, one that is unlike many others. We were born in the same town and met in church nursery school. We went on to graduate kindergarten, elementary school, high school, and even college together.

The elementary school Darla and I attended made a big deal about kindergarten graduation with caps, gowns, tassels, and even diplomas! On our "graduation" day, we were having our class picture taken and the teacher put me in my usual place—front row, center—where she could keep an eye on me. As I stood there waiting for the photo to be taken, very proud in my cap and gown, I glanced to my left. Beside me stood a little girl with long dark hair, big brown eyes, and skin tanned to a golden brown. I thought, *She's kinda cute.*

She looked back at me—tall, skinny, red-haired, freckle-faced, with knobby knees—and thought to herself, *He's kind of a geek.*

As the years passed, she got cuter and I got geekier. And I'm proud to say on July 30, 1983, I married that cute little girl and promised to love her for the rest of my life.

Darla and I started married life with many things in common. We shared a community, common upbringings, and a common faith. According to research, we started out with pretty good odds for success. But many times I've thought, *July 30, 1983.* It is my way of reflecting on our incredible ignorance as we stood at the altar over 20 years ago. We vowed to love each other for better or for worse, for richer or poorer, in sickness and in health. We said the words, and we meant the words, but we didn't understand the words. We didn't have a clue about how much work was ahead of us.

Life in today's world is tough and seems to be getting tougher. Marriage in our world is tough and seems to be getting tougher. So we have a choice to make. We can complain about the difficulties or we can embrace them. We can pat ourselves on the back and walk away from a difficult marriage feeling that we did our best but it simply wasn't meant to be. Or we can tap into the hero within and face difficulties in marriage with uncommon courage, exceptional attitude, and unyielding dignity. Of course, that is easier said than done.

When Lucas was recovering from full spinal fusion surgery, he had to fight for his life several times. I remember looking at his unresponsive little body and kissing him good-bye as they wheeled him away for a second surgery. Darla and I were completely wiped out physically and emotionally. When we sat down together in the surgical waiting room, again I thought, *July 30, 1983.* Moments like that, like those we've faced over and over with Lucas, never even entered my mind on our wedding day.

Marriage is naturally stressful. It can involve financial stress, the stress of raising kids, the stress of daily demands on your time and energy, and the stress of living with someone else's quirks. These are

common frustrations every family faces, but adding a child with disabilities dramatically increases the tension in a marriage.

Facing the reality of parenting a disabled child greatly
increased the stress factor in our marriage. Though we've always
been comfortable financially, Lucas's birth created obvious financial
stress due to the cost of medications, full-time medical care, frequent emergency room visits, and extended stays in intensive care.

In addition to financial pressure, our emotional stress has gone
through the roof at times. We didn't anticipate parenting a child
with severe disabilities, yet there he was. We've had to deal with the
fear of the unknown as well as the fear of the known. Add in pro-
longed times of separation, when one parent is staying at the hospital with Lucas while the other is caring for the boys at home, and
anyone would agree that our emotional well-being has been taxed.

We've been bombarded with the physical stress of fatigue.
Many nights have been virtually void of sleep after waking to the
sound of monitors, administering medications, managing seizures,
or simply checking to see if our son was still breathing.

The birth of Lucas has also created spiritual stress, leading us
to question God tirelessly at times: What's the purpose? Why
Lucas? Why us? At times the spiritual strain has driven us to our
knees in prayer and to the Scriptures for comfort. At other times
it has driven us away from God, even causing us to question His
existence. Ultimately it has deepened our faith, making us stronger
through adversity, but it has often been a painful process.

When I coached basketball, my teams became very familiar
with the words, "focus, focus, focus." If we could just focus for
eight minutes a quarter, four quarters at a time, then we would
have a great chance of winning the game. Focus, focus, focus for
thirty-two minutes of every game on executing the plan and

employing the fundamentals. It's no different in the "game" of marriage. Focus, focus, focus—every day, whether apart or together, executing God's plan and employing the fundamentals. We must choose to focus on living as one flesh, indivisible, with Christ as the head of our homes. Focus, focus, focus every day on serving one another and putting the cause above ourselves and our spouses and children above ourselves, because a healthy marriage truly resembles a winning team.

A team is two or more people coming together to accomplish a common goal. It is safe to assume that a couple, on their wedding day, shares the common goal of loving one another for a lifetime. So what makes them give up on that goal? They lose focus. They begin focusing on the good of the individual rather than the good of the team. It doesn't work in basketball games, and it won't work in marriage. Winning teams are made up of individuals focused on earning the trust of their teammates and willing to serve one another. They value self-sacrifice, and they realize that rising above obstacles will make victories even sweeter. When a good team wins, it celebrates individual successes. When a good team loses, the members shoulder the loss together, each assessing his or her own contribution to the failure and never pointing fingers.

Winning teams stay focused. They see the end in sight. They see the goal. And the "end" is what drives them.

A winning marriage stays focused on the goal. It is driven by the desire, the goal, to leave a positive legacy for the next generation. Winning marriage partners refuse to focus on the good of the individual and are determined to pursue the good of the team. They find the strength to endure, because they dare to dream about the good that can be accomplished.

We should approach our marriages as we would a basketball

game. We should dream together. We should encourage one another. We should work hard together. We should believe that success is possible even in the face of adversity. And we should remind each other often of the goal. Some of the best basketball games have been won in the final seconds, by teams who fought from behind to take the lead. Never were the best basketball games played by teams that gave up at halftime.

God's Word explains how a husband is to accept the role of coach and fulfill the responsibility of creating teamwork in the home. In Ephesians 5:25 we read, "Husbands, love your wives, just as Christ loved the church and gave himself up for her." Men, we are told to love our wives as Christ loves the church. Wow! Christ loved the church so much that He died for it. His own people—His church—spat on Him, beat Him, and called Him names. They wished Him nothing but harm, yet He said, "Father, forgive them" (Luke 23:34). Do I love my wife with that kind of love? Do you love your spouse with that kind of love? God expects you to defend your wife, not condemn her. You are expected to protect her, cherish her, and present her without blemish.

We are taught that husbands are to love their wives as they love their own bodies (see Ephesians 5:28-29). There is an enormous responsibility on the shoulders of men. And men must rise to the challenge if they want their marriages to succeed. If we want to leave legacies our children will be proud of, we must become leaders of our households. Not in a heavy-handed manner, but as servants.

I have dropped the ball many times in our marriage, using my leadership role as a tool of power rather than one of service. I married the right person, but I believe I married her when I was too young and too immature to understand the magnitude of my role as a husband. Early in our marriage, life was all about me—not about us—and not at all about being the leader of a winning team. I was selfish and self-indulgent.

Thank God He used Darla to help me grow and that He has blessed and protected our marriage over the years. I love Darla deeply, but I haven't always acted lovingly toward her. I've had to learn to love her and our boys sacrificially, with the heart of a servant, the heart of Christ. It's a calling no man can ever perfect. It's a lifelong process that can be incredibly difficult some days, but it's a process we must embrace if we are focused on leaving a legacy of leadership and integrity.

The most heroic thing moms and dads can do is to love one another, putting cause above self. When we put our marriages above ourselves, our kids above ourselves, society above ourselves, and our country above ourselves, then we are learning to love heroically.

The Bible tells us that love bears all things, believes all things, hopes all things, and endures all things (see 1 Corinthians 13:7). Though Lucas has brought a tremendous amount of stress into our marriage and family, his presence has also taught us the essence of true love. He has taught us the importance of pulling together as a couple in the midst of chaos and pain and to focus, focus, focus.

Darla and I have had to focus on creating a winning team. Focusing on the inconvenience and stress would have torn our marriage apart years ago. More than 20 years later, I still reflect on the date, "July 30, 1983." We didn't have a clue. In many ways, we still don't have a clue, and that's okay. It's okay that we don't know what's on our horizon, because we know we are committed to one another. We want to be in the ranks of married heroes. We want our lives together to speak to the next generation, saying that for better or worse we are one in Christ until death do us part.

♦ ♦   ♦ ♦   ♦ ♦   ♦ ♦   ♦ ♦   ♦ ♦   ♦ ♦   ♦ ♦   ♦ ♦   ♦ ♦

Dear Lucas,

It was great to see you today. Your brothers, Ruth, and I had a great time being with you. Your mom wishes she could have joined us, but there were things at home that needed her attention.

Mom's absence made me think about your future. I don't always miss your mom when she's not with me, but today I did. For some reason, it made me think of what life would be like if I weren't married. Your mom is my life-partner and my best friend.

I love your mom and she loves me. Although I knew your mom was pretty the first time I saw her, today she is the most beautiful person I know.

Mom and I are fortunate. We have grown more in love with one another through our years of marriage. And I believe your life was the impetus for this growth. We didn't know where to turn after you were born, so we turned to each other. Then we turned to God. It's true that when there is nowhere to run and nowhere to hide, you find God. In our case, we rediscovered each other in the process of seeking Him.

You won't experience marriage, but your life makes our marriage better. You will not have children of your own, but your life has a positive impact on parents. You will not run, jump, or play like other children, but you inspire athletes and those of us who are "normal" to maximize our potential and give thanks for our abilities.

Your future will certainly look different from that of other boys your age, but your life provides unique perspective and motivation that will make the futures of others more dynamic.

God has used your life to help me fall more deeply in love with your mom. Along with uncertainty and complexity, your life brings us abundant love and joy. You have drawn us closer to God and closer to one another.

I'm sorry you will never experience a first date, or prom night, or the love of a spouse, but take heart in knowing your life has multiplied our love and made our marriage and our family more beautiful.

I love you, kid.

Dad

Chapter Nine

Leadership Isn't Optional

Sitting in the office of one of my mentors, a man who spent many years as an educator and then as the chief executive officer of an organization serving people with disabilities, I asked how I might better understand Lucas, how I could be a more effective father to Lucas, and how Darla and I could be certain we were doing everything possible to give Lucas the best quality of life.

After listening patiently to my concerns about parenting a disabled son, my friend responded with a message I hadn't anticipated but which I will never forget. Though my questions were all about Lucas, his answers were not. Instead, he addressed the parental responsibility Darla and I have to our "normal" children. I was intrigued as he talked with me about a common pitfall of parents in our situation.

He explained that when a child with disabilities enters a family, the focus tends to shift entirely to the needs of that child, leaving siblings feeling slighted. Healthy children often get lost in the shuffle of daily demands, their needs gradually taking a backseat to those of their disabled sibling. The message my friend delivered that day was this: As you focus on loving Lucas and serving his needs, do not overlook the needs of your other children. He was challenging Darla and me to be intentional in the way we parent each of our boys, not just Lucas.

When calling ambulances, coordinating medical treatments,

and simply adjusting to the emotion of caring for a child with disabilities, it's very easy for time and energy to be consumed. During Lucas's first six years, our family was divided many times. Darla would stay at home with Lucas while I took Hans and Josh to a ball game. Or I'd stay home with Lucas while Darla took the rest of the family to church. We often attended family gatherings separately so one of us could stay home to care for Lucas. It was becoming a way of life, and the advice of our friend caused us to examine the parental attitudes and actions we were developing.

It was this examination that was largely responsible for our decision to transition Lucas from our home to the full-time care of CCHS. The specialized care that Lucas required had grown beyond our expertise, and we believed that settling him into a specialized care facility was the right decision for him. We also believed, however, that moving Lucas was the right decision for Hans, Josh, and Logan.

Not only were we able to spend more unified time as a family, we began taking weekly family trips to visit Lucas. At least once a week we piled into the family Suburban, driving an hour and a half to spend the day with Lucas. These have become treasured moments, with little interruption or outside interference, and God has used them to bring our family closer together.

As I have pondered the message of my mentor over the years, I've come to the conclusion that the essence of our success as parents doesn't lie in proven methods, but simply in our determination to leave something of value behind. Success is found when we are intentional about the way we approach every moment of our lives.

Deuteronomy 6:5-9 reminds us to "love the Lord your God with all your heart and with all your soul and with all your strength. These commandments that I give you today are to be upon your hearts. Impress them on your children. Talk about them when you sit at home and when you walk along the road, when you lie down and when you get up. Tie them as symbols on your hands and bind them on your foreheads. Write them on the doorframes of your houses and on your gates."

First things first: Love the Lord your God. Then, talk about Him in the ordinary moments—all the time. When you sit at the dining room table or drive in the car. When you go to bed at night or when you're getting ready in the morning. Every day, every moment, let your kids see that you love the Lord with all your heart, soul, and strength. Let them see it in the words you speak and the decisions you make.

We've spent many hours visiting with Hans, Josh, and Logan about the journey of Lucas. We've talked openly about the decision and struggle of moving Lucas to a full-time facility. We've talked with them about the fact that they may be responsible to care for their brother someday, when Darla and I are gone. We've talked to them about loving Lucas as a member of our family even though he doesn't live in our home.

Not only have our boys grown to love Lucas deeply, they have developed a love and concern for others with special needs. For Darla and me, the best part about parent-teacher conferences isn't the *academic* report but the *compassion* report. It gives us great joy to hear that our children are quick to reach out to classmates who are being teased or who need a helping hand. And I believe they have learned to be compassionate because they've seen others show compassion for Lucas.

They've learned that Lucas is valuable to our family simply because he is their brother, not because of what he looks like or what he has to offer. When we take Lucas to a public event, such as a basketball game, our kids are never embarrassed by him. Lucas has helped us leave a legacy of compassion, teaching our boys to love the unlovely and to serve those with special needs as Christ did.

Every situation in our day is a tool, a legacy-building tool. We can take advantage of ordinary moments, grabbing hold of them to show our children how to live lives of integrity, or we can simply get through the day. Each of us has a choice. We can leave a legacy of excellence or of mediocrity.

My dad lost his parents in a car accident when he was 13 years old. He was the oldest child in the family, and he was required to fend for himself. It would have been easy for him to be angry with God and resent his circumstances, but he didn't. He chose to focus on making something of himself and seeking God's purpose for his life.

My parents have had to bury three of their children: an infant, a six-year-old, and a young adult. Despite incredible heartache my parents often express gratitude for the time they had, thankful that God entrusted them with these three children even though their time on earth was short. Of course, we saw our parents grieve. They have experienced a range of emotion over the years, but they have continually expressed an attitude of acceptance of God's timing and His sovereignty.

The lessons I learned simply by watching and listening to my parents react to the situations in their lives have been invaluable. Whether in extraordinary moments or ordinary ones, my parents taught me the importance of turning to God when dealing with difficult circumstances.

True colors are displayed in the midst of adversity. How do you respond when things don't go your way? In these moments we are shaping the next generation. I believe the verses in Deuteronomy are teaching us the way to leave an excellent legacy. They teach us to intentionally talk with our kids about the everyday stuff of life. The things that are passed from generation to generation are the things rehearsed in our homes on good days and difficult days, and we leave a positive legacy when our daily habits reflect that we love the Lord with all of our heart, soul, and strength.

Ronald Reagan is one of my heroes. Obviously, he left our country a great legacy through his service as governor of California and then as president. He inspired many through the way he lived and the passion with which he spoke, but no people were more touched by his life than his own children.

The day of Ronald Reagan's funeral it was heartwarming to hear his children pay tribute to their dad—not Governor Reagan, not President Reagan—just Dad. They talked about how he prepared them for his death, assuring them that he would be in heaven because he knew Jesus Christ as his Savior. They talked about the way his life reflected the love he had for God.

When his daughter, Patti, gave her eulogy she told a precious story of how her father used an ordinary moment to teach a valuable life lesson. This was her reflection:

> [My dad] was the one who generously offered funeral services for my goldfish on the morning of its demise. We went out into the garden and dug a tiny grave with a teaspoon, and he took two twigs and lashed them together with twine and formed a cross as a marker for the grave. And then he gave a beautiful eulogy.
>
> He told me that my fish was swimming in the clear blue waters in heaven, and he would never tire, and he would never get hungry, and he would never be in any danger, and he could swim as far and wide as he wanted, and he never had to stop, because the river went on forever. He was free.

When we went back inside and I looked at my remaining goldfish in their aquarium with their pink plastic castle and their colored rocks, I suggested that perhaps we should kill the others so they could also go to that clear blue river and be free.

He then took more time out of his morning—I'm sure he actually did have other things to do that day—and patiently explained to me that in God's time, the other fish would go there, as well. In God's time, we would all be taken home. And even though it sometimes seemed a mystery, we were just asked to trust that God's time was right and wise.[7]

What a powerful legacy Ronald Reagan left for his daughter, a legacy that doesn't fear death but embraces the idea of eternity with anticipation. Through the death of a goldfish, he taught her that all life has value, that heaven is a place of beauty, and that God's timing is perfect even when it doesn't make sense to us. If he would have simply flushed the dead goldfish, he would have robbed his daughter of a treasured lesson, one that gave her great comfort at the time of his own death and one that is now being passed on to the next generation.

When Hans was 17 years old, the two of us attended a men's conference together. Much of the information we were given that weekend wasn't new to us. In fact, it wasn't the information that challenged me. The challenge was in knowing my teenage son was a witness to the information I was receiving. I knew he would be watching me as we returned home to see if my life would reflect the principles we were taught at the conference. Whether he knew it or not, he would be taking notes: Is my dad truly a promise keeper? When things don't go his way, does my dad still follow God's principles?

In our fast-paced, professional world people often say, "It's not what you know, it's who you know." Though I understand the concept, I believe it goes one step further. It's not what you know and it's not who you know, but it's what you know about who you know. We are hungry for authenticity. We want people's actions to reflect their words. In reality, our names, titles, and bank accounts are far less meaningful than the way we live our daily lives.

In 2 Corinthians 3:1-3 Paul writes, "Are we beginning to commend ourselves again? Or do we need, like some people, letters of recommendation to you or from you? You yourselves are our letter, written on our hearts, known and read by everybody . . . written not with ink but with the Spirit of the living God, not on tablets of stone but on tablets of human hearts."

Paul tells us to cut to the chase. It doesn't matter what we say about ourselves. It doesn't matter what others say about us. It doesn't matter how many votes we get or what is written in our résumés. The only thing that matters is what people learn when they read the letters of our lives. What do they see? What's important? What isn't?

Mom, you are a letter. Dad, you are a letter. Teacher, boss, grandparent, high school student—each of you is a letter. Your life is read by the world. Does it say that you love God with all your heart, soul, and strength? Does it say that your words match your actions, or does it say that you're a hypocrite?

There are days when I don't want people to read my letter. I'd rather not be proofed by the world. But most days, viewing my life as a letter gives me great energy and inspiration. If my life is an open book, I want to keep my focus where the focus needs to be. I want to be intentional about leaving a legacy.

When Lucas was at the University of Iowa Hospital, I had the opportunity to visualize the passing-on of a legacy. Lucas had gone into a severe state of distress. Darla and I were in his hospital room as it filled with medical staff. Nurses were shouting out orders and machines were shouting out warning signals. We began encouraging the doctors and nurses, talking to Lucas, and praying that God would spare the life of our son.

As I took hold of Lucas's hand, I glanced toward the doorway. There they stood, in staircase formation, just outside the hospital room. Hans, Josh, and Logan were staring intensely into the room of their brother, looking like his guardian angels. They had all seen Lucas in crisis situations before, but this time I was keenly aware that they were watching me and watching Darla. They were observing our words, attitudes, and actions, and they were taking mental notes. I remember thinking, *What message are we sending? What legacy are we leaving?* It was a picture of generation to generation. I knew those moments would stay with them for the rest of their lives and likely be passed on to their children.

Over the years, I have mastered the art of multitasking while driving (an "art" that is neither safe nor recommended). When I'm driving with a cup of coffee in my hand and the cell phone rings, I pick up the phone with my "free" hand, put it to my mouth, pull the antenna up with my teeth, flip the phone open with my fingers, and punch the answer button with my thumb, never taking my eyes off the road or letting go of my coffee mug. It's a habit. I do it without even thinking about the process.

One Saturday when Josh and I were on our way home from a basketball practice, my phone rang. Instead of picking up the phone myself, I asked Josh to answer it. He had both hands free but without hesitation he picked up the phone with one hand, put it up to his mouth, pulled the antenna up with his teeth, flipped it open with his fingers, and punched the answer button with his thumb. I was speechless.

Most of the time it isn't so visible, but every now and then God gives us a glimpse of the legacy we're leaving. When I saw my children standing in staircase formation, watching me from the hospital hallway, it was a snapshot of how closely my children observe me in the extraordinary moments. When I saw Josh answer my phone exactly as I do, it was a snapshot of how closely my children observe me in the ordinary moments. Every moment, simple or grand, our kids are looking and watching. What are they seeing?

When Logan sees me putting on a tie, he frequently asks, "Who you speaking to tonight, Dad?" It's as if he is saying, "I know who you are, Dad. I know what you love to do. I'm watching you. And I'm learning."

Some day, on my deathbed, I hope to say, "I have fought the good fight, I have finished the race, I have kept the faith. Now there is in store for me the crown of righteousness, which the Lord, the righteous Judge, will award to me on that day" (2 Timothy 4:7-8). More importantly, though, I hope my boys will be able to say that about me.

I hope the ordinary moments I've shared with them have taught them to live lives of integrity, passion, and faith. I hope I will have handled the extraordinary moments in such a way that inspires them to be men of character. And most of all, I hope they will find great comfort in knowing I am in heaven, in the presence of the Holy God, not because of my performance on earth but because I believed in Christ's sacrifice for my sin.

When I tuck Logan into bed at night, I say, "I love you, Logan."

He says, "I love you too, Dad."

"I like you, Logan."

"I like you too, Dad."

"You're the best, Logan."

"Nah, we're both the best, Dad."

The success of our lives is ultimately determined by the legacy we leave behind. Eighteenth-century author Johann von Schiller wrote, "He who has done his best for his own time has lived for all times."[8] Each of us has the privilege and responsibility of impacting those who come after us. We must choose, in ordinary moments and extraordinary ones, to be intentional about leaving a legacy of excellence for the next generation.

A LETTER TO LUCAS, FROM OUR OLDEST SON, HANS

Dear Lucas,

When people ask who has been the most influential person in my life, I never have to stop and think. Without a doubt, you are the one who has crafted the way I view my life and the lives of others. After hearing my answer, those same people usually ask how a person who cannot talk can have such significant influence or teach in any way. Well, quite frankly, those people don't know you. I think that every person who has met you has been changed because of you.

I have often wondered why God made you the way you are. I've had feelings of sadness and anger but mostly just confusion. I couldn't find any reason why you were created with such severe disabilities when the Bible says that everyone is made perfectly. For the longest time, I couldn't find God's perfection in you and it gave me doubts. Being a teenager, I know all about doubts. When you're younger, everything is black and white and easy, but as you grow older, a lot of things turn gray. Things that used to seem clear begin to turn upside down in your mind, and you find yourself wondering about them.

In my case, I began to wonder whether or not God is real. I never told Mom or Dad this, but that question stayed on my mind for a long time. I'd gone to church with our family since I was a baby and had been told by every significant person in my life that God is real, as if it was something that required no thought. I could see this beautifully created world, with God's fingerprints all over it. Yet I could also see the terrible things in this world and I just had so many questions: Why was Lucas created this way? Why did my friend Archie have to get in that accident and become paralyzed? If there is so much abortion and so many unwanted babies in this world, then why doesn't God give a baby to Eric and Jenilyn, a couple who would make awesome parents? On a more of a global scale, why is there always war? Why do innocent kids die of disease and starvation all over the world?

Well, Lucas, I know I'll never have the answers to all my questions, but because of you, I don't have to. What I used to see as imperfection in you now looks like perfection. You are the example. You live the way we are all supposed to live.

You have it worse than any other person I know, yet you smile more than any person I know. You can't do any of the things that "normal" people can do, but you never feel sorry for yourself. To be honest, you amaze me. If I suddenly found myself in your condition, I wouldn't even want to live, but you're the happiest person I know. You go into a violent seizure and come out of it laughing. I don't get it.

My own "huge problems" are nothing compared to yours, but I still get downhearted more often than you. I get stressed over a fight with a girl, while you come out of near-death experiences unfazed. Once again, I don't get it.

You change me every time I see you, Lucas. For all these reasons, you continue to influence me and make me better.

More than anything, I feel God's presence when I'm with you. I can't really explain it, I just know. You may not be able to talk, but you are a great witness. You make me realize that God has a purpose for everything, though we may never understand it, and it's okay if we don't because He is God and we are not.

Thanks for everything, Lucas. I love you.

Hans

Chapter Ten

It's Not for Us to Understand

Our society thrives on change—the newest, most improved, and never-seen-anything-like-it-before. We are conditioned to find ways to better our homes, our bodies, our intellects, and our careers. We enjoy change, but we want it on our terms. We want the fairy tale. We want control. In fact, in our self-driven world we have become writers of our own destinies, confident in our own abilities to determine and deliver what is best. We accept change when it feels good. But when change is unexpected or painful, when we hit a bump in the road—or a crater—it often leaves us feeling insecure—full of questions, frustration, and stress.

In January 1996 Darla and I were living in Sheldon with our three young boys; I was the Sheldon High School principal. Our life there was familiar and secure. We were very content with our circumstances, not looking for a change, when I received an offer to become the CEO of Opportunities Unlimited (OU), a non-profit organization serving people with disabilities. Not only would this mean a change in career path, but also the need to relocate our family to Sioux City. The pros and cons list was well in favor of staying in Sheldon. There were so many reasons to stay and so few reasons to go, but we couldn't deny the prompting we felt to go for it, to leave behind the comfort and security that we knew and move to Sioux City.

The potential of OU's mission inspired me, yet the organization was on a fast downward spiral: issued 54 pages of state deficiencies—not 54 items, but 54 pages. It was in need of corporate CPR.

I love a challenge, so I rolled up my sleeves determined to deliver a success story. It wasn't long before the reality of the situation set in. While we were making progress clinically, we were definitely day-to-day financially. Less than six weeks after taking the helm, a board member advised me to keep my career options open, signaling the corporation's ongoing concern. In addition to the clinical and financial hurdles that needed to be cleared, the office building was in a less-than-desirable location, making safety a concern. And in an ongoing effort to implement a culture committed to fulfilling OU's mission with excellence, I made daily determinations of who would stay on the team and who would be made available for employment elsewhere. These decisions were not easy, as I knew they had life-altering implications.

Any job change creates stress, but I gave up a job with a dependable paycheck and government funding in exchange for a 60-minute commute (each way), to work for an organization that may or may not survive the week. Major stress!

Darla and I began to scout real estate listings for a house in Sioux City and to prepare our home in Sheldon for sale. Relocating a family of five is no simple task. We eventually decided to purchase two acres of land, tucked into the beautiful rolling hills of Sioux City's northeast side, and build a new house. After all, we were not going to have any more children, so we were ready to spend some money and brain power creating the perfect home for our family, a home complete with the amenities necessary to accommodate Lucas's special needs.

Pouring myself into the restoration of OU was an inspiring challenge, demanding an incredible measure of mental and emotional energy. In addition, our three boys still needed their dad to be fully engaged. We were continually adjusting to Lucas's disabilities, trying to keep up with Hans's and Josh's activities, and making the many arrangements and decisions that come with building a new home. My life was full. Or at least I thought it was, until Darla called me at the office one day to announce that she was pregnant! I remember asking God, "Why? I left a job and community I loved because You prompted me to do it, and You reward me now with a pregnant wife?" Major stress!

Eight months later our little, white tornado was born. He is named Logan but affectionately called "payback" by my parents. Logan was an unexpected blessing, and his arrival brought a great deal of healing to our family. He was the little brother that Hans and Josh could play with, and he completed things for Lucas too, giving him brothers in front and behind. Only God knew what we really needed and what we were capable of handling. Isaiah 55:9 says, "As the heavens are higher than the earth, so are my ways higher than your ways and my thoughts than your thoughts." In my limited, human understanding I thought another child would simply be a burden, one more thing consuming my time and money. In God's abundant wisdom, He knew that Logan would not be a burden at all but would bring the kind of joy and vitality I didn't even realize I needed.

During that season of life, we were forced to embrace change over and over again. Some of it was by our own choosing and some was not. Some of it was frightening and some of it exhilarating, but God used each situation to show me, in a very tangible way, that He is in control and He knows what is best.

Fast-forward to April 30, 2004. Lucas was now 10 years old and had been in the hospital, in and out of intensive care, for nearly a month following spinal fusion surgery. Because the hospital was 75 miles from our home, Darla stayed with Lucas while I stayed in Sioux City to care for Hans, Josh, and Logan. Darla's tireless devotion during those difficult days was a tribute to motherhood. She wanted to stay with Lucas, but we both knew she needed a break, so we arranged to switch roles for a couple of days.

My first day at the hospital was a good one. Lucas was doing well and I enjoyed being by his side, kissing his head and singing his favorite songs. That evening I made my bed on the pull-out couch in his room and finally fell asleep shortly after midnight—just in time to be awakened by his cries. Thinking he simply needed to be changed or repositioned, I ventured into the brightly lit hospital hallway to ask for assistance.

Moments later two nurses began working with Lucas to determine what was making him uncomfortable and they quickly discovered his IV line had blown. They informed me a new line would have to be started, disappointing news because he had extremely small veins, turning a simple procedure into a tedious and painful event. The flight technician came and began the process of starting the IV. I tried to help by holding Lucas's head in my hands, distracting him from the repeated pricks and pokes to his arm and keeping his eyes fixed on me. As they continued working on him, he became totally silent—too silent. I looked at his chest. It wasn't moving. I studied his face. He wasn't breathing. I felt his skin. It was burning up.

In the midst of a sudden outbreak of activity, I backed away as they ceased their efforts with the IV and put a breathing bag over

Lucas's nose and mouth to resuscitate him. Once he was breathing again, they took his temperature: 105.7 degrees. Before I could process the situation they were rushing him to the intensive care unit, still trying to start the IV.

Do I call Darla? The question repeated in my mind when one of the nurses instructed me to call her. It was the middle of the night. Darla would have to drive 90 minutes, all alone, to get to the hospital. But I knew the nurse was right; I had to call. Darla was already awake when the phone rang, feeling she should be in Sioux Falls with Lucas. When she arrived at the hospital, she described her emotional trip and miles of passionate, honest discussion with God as she yelled her frustration through tears.

Lucas's tiny veins kept collapsing, making it nearly impossible to start the IV that was so vitally needed. He was enveloped in cooling blankets, but his temperature kept rising. Finally, just before Darla arrived, they were able to access one of the carotids and get him stabilized. At 4:00 A.M. I found a spot to lie down and was able to sleep until Darla woke me a few hours later, telling me that his temperature had climbed to 106.9 degrees. Again, I went to his side, held his head in my hands, and talked to him. We had been through many critical situations with Lucas, but it never became easy. It was so difficult to see him connected to machines, with cords coming and going from his body, looking so lifeless. Moments later, he began having a major seizure and I thought, "This is it."

Despite my fears, the medical team was able to get him stabilized once again. Our nerves were running thin and emotions running high when we received a much-needed answer to prayer. As if from nowhere on that Saturday morning, an entire surgical team appeared outside Lucas's door. There was the surgeon with his gown on, his assistant, and all the professionals needed to make and carry out the decision to reopen and irrigate Lucas's incision—flushing out the staph infection that had taken up residence in his back.

Darla and I started down the hallway with Lucas and the medical team, accompanying them to the operating room. As we stood in the elevator, the intensive care nurse began reporting Lucas's vital statistics to the surgical nurse. When she reported his temperature to be 107 degrees, the surgical nurse must have forgotten that we were present, and said, "Oh my God!" It sent a chill down my spine, and again I thought, "This is it."

As we sat in the waiting room, Darla and I began to plan a funeral, yet prayed that God would allow him to survive the surgery. God answered that prayer, and Lucas began a very slow and rocky recovery.

As parents we instinctively fought for the life of our child, yet there were moments in that waiting room when, in my human understanding, it made sense for God to take Lucas while he was under anesthetic, without pain or fear. In heaven he will be fully restored, allowing him to run, sing, and play. It made sense to me that streets of pure gold and seas of crystal will be far better for him than ICU hallways and IV needles. God's ways are higher than our ways, His thoughts higher than our thoughts, and He always knows what is best, even when we don't understand.

When I returned to work on Monday, I was met with painful irony. I learned a woman in our community had been jogging when she was hit and killed by a pickup truck. She and her husband had been deeply in love, with a marriage that inspired other couples. She was a stay-at-home mom, happily devoted to their four young children. The questions were relentless: Why would God allow this beloved wife and mother to be killed, yet sustain the life of Lucas? Why are old men and women lying in nursing homes, wishing to die, and yet they live? Lucas touched death many times, reaching out his hand as if to say, "Here I am, God," yet his life was spared.

Why? Because God's thoughts are higher than our thoughts, His ways are higher than our ways, and it's not for us to understand.

Even Jesus grieved. He grieved at the thought of his own death (Luke 22:42-44) and He grieved the death of His friend (John 11:33-36). Surely Jesus had an intimate understanding of the mind of His heavenly Father, yet He still experienced sorrow and pain. People often say they have a list of questions to ask God when they get to heaven, but when we actually get there and see Him face-to-face—when we see the whole of His plan in place—maybe we will simply say, "Of course, now it all makes sense." When we are in His presence, able to focus on Him, our questions may become suddenly insignificant.

When we took our boys to visit my sister Kay in Michigan, she took us to the local mall, which has a massive rock-climbing wall. Now, being Dutch, I don't part with money easily, but we were on vacation and I was feeling generous, so I told the boys we would pay for them to climb the wall. Logan, our little white tornado, was the only one to accept the challenge. He was six years old and fearless. He had been observing as teenagers and adults alike attempted to reach the top, lost their grip, and fell away from the wall at the same protruding point. But Logan was ready to go!

As they were strapping on his harness, he looked up at me and asked if I was planning to climb with him. "Unh-uh. I'm not climbing any wall," I said, "but I'll be right here to encourage you and talk you through it." A few moments later he was on his way up and I was cheering him on. "Hey, good job, Logan! Push off with your left foot. Now reach up with your right hand. Grab on. Hold on tight."

Darla and Aunt Kay's cameras were working overtime and, to my surprise, Logan was doing pretty well. As he reached the section of the wall that had defeated most adults, he grabbed on tight, trying to move to safety, but suddenly let go. The belt around his small body suspended him far above our heads, inches from the wall. I thought, *Oh, well, it was a good attempt, but that's it.* What impressed me is that Logan never looked away. He never looked down. He just stared at the wall, reached for it, and persisted climbing. I stood there, looking up at him, thinking, *You stud!*

He continued climbing until he reached the top, giving it a slap of victory. I started yelling, "That's my son!" Later as we waited for them to remove his harness, we discussed his accomplishment. Why could Logan, a scrawny six-year-old, conquer the wall when teenagers and adults were unable to do so? Darla assessed it beautifully saying, "Because he has incredible focus when he chooses to apply it."

We are all climbing every day through this rocky journey called life. We encounter obstacles along the way that require us to change course; we experience pain and fear, confusion, and stress. Because life's journey is full of detours and situations that are difficult to understand, we must choose to focus on that which can be understood. During these stressful times our minds may not be able to comprehend the "why," but we can find peace in embracing the sovereignty of God, believing His grace is boundless and His wisdom is supreme.

God knows we are incapable of perfection and our struggle with sin will never be over until we leave this earth, but "because of his great love for us, God, who is rich in mercy, made us alive with Christ even when we were dead in transgressions. . . . For it is by grace you have been saved, through faith—and this not from yourselves, it is the gift of God" (Ephesians 2:4-5, 8). What a wonderful truth! No matter how inconvenient or traumatic our situation, God loves us and sent His Son to save us from the eternal damnation we deserve. If the rest of our earthly existence was plagued with pain, the gift of His saving grace should be enough reason to press on with joy in our hearts.

Not only can we focus on God's grace, but His mighty power. For Joshua, God stopped the sun "in the middle of the sky and delayed [its] going down about a full day" (Joshua 10:13). For the Israelites, He divided the waters of the Red Sea so they were able to pass through "on dry ground, with a wall of water on their right and on their left" (Exodus 14: 21-22). For you and me, He overcame the power of death, raising Jesus from the dead and "freeing him from the agony of death, because it was impossible for death to keep its hold on him" (Acts 2:24).

When we stop to ponder the wonder of His power, we must also recognize His ability to fix our problems in the blink of an eye. So if He is able to shield us from pain, from the heartache of loss and the stress of uncertainty, then why does He allow us to suffer? He allows us times of suffering because, in His omnipotence, He knows more than we know and sees more than we see. God promises to work the details of our lives together for good (Romans 8:28), even when it makes no sense to us. He "rain[ed] down bread from heaven" when His children were hungry (Exodus 16:4) and made drinking water come out of a rock to quench their thirst (Exodus 17:6). We must choose to focus on the fact that He is able, if it is for our good.

We must trust His supreme wisdom. God has an incomprehensible knowledge of the past, present, and future and an intimate knowledge of your life and mine. It's as though we are only capable of one-dimensional, black-and-white judgments, but His decisions are made in 3-D and full color.

When a two-year-old tries to touch a hot stove, his parent will certainly intervene, instructing the child that the burner is hot and will burn him if he persists. The child remains intrigued, unconvinced of the danger, and continues reaching. The parent continues to act in the best interest of the child, abruptly pulling him away from the danger, and the child is left feeling deprived and unfulfilled even though he should be feeling grateful and relieved. This scenario is simple, producing little argument, but isn't this duplicated in our adult lives when we experience circumstances that leave us feeling deprived, unfulfilled, and even unloved? Sometimes we must simply trust God's wisdom above our own.

Whatever we focus on fervently is the thing that will rule us. When we choose to focus on our problems, we wind up frustrated and depressed. When we focus on our own ability to control our circumstances, we are left feeling worried and helpless. When we focus on that which we wish we had, we are consumed by feelings of deprivation. What would happen if we decided today to fervently focus on God and His Word? What would happen if we forced ourselves to view our problems and insufficiencies through a divine filter and to surrender our need for control?

From the first moment Lucas entered the world, it was painfully evident that Darla and I were powerless to "fix" him. His life journey has caused us to experience the gamut of emotion and has taught us to pray, "Thy will be done."

Jesus didn't enjoy suffering. He didn't enjoy being spat upon, or whipped, or nailed to a cross. He didn't want to experience the pain He knew was looming, so He prayed, "My Father, if it is possible, may this cup be taken from me" (Matthew 26:39). But He chose to trust and focus on God's wisdom rather than His own comfort. Because He chose to focus on the incredible love in His heart for you and me, He was able to pray, "If it is not possible for this cup to be taken away unless I drink it, may your will be done" (Matthew 26:42). He trusted His Father's heart, even when His circumstances were frightening and uncomfortable.

We would not have chosen a son with disabilities. We never wanted to spend endless nights in the intensive care unit, holding the head of our child as he fought to take another breath. But it has given us a crash course in embracing God's sovereignty. When we focus on Lucas's disabilities and deficiencies, we feel angry and afraid, but when we focus on God's grace, power, and wisdom, we find the strength to earnestly thank God for the opportunity to know Lucas, just as he is—to hold him and to love him. The quality of our lives, in response to Lucas, has depended on our focus. We have learned to trust God even when we don't understand, and to apply the words of this simple chorus:

Turn your eyes upon Jesus,
Look full in His wonderful face,
And the things of earth will grow strangely dim,
In the light of His glory and grace.

Dear Lucas,

There is so much I don't understand.

I don't understand why women have to suffer during childbirth, while men simply watch.

I don't understand why so many athletes with natural, God-given abilities have such low ambition.

I don't understand why some couples are blessed with many children while others remain barren.

I don't understand why some children are abused by their own parents.

I don't understand why some people are abundantly blessed while others are in a constant state of struggle.

I don't understand why you and I get to live in America while others suffer in third-world countries.

I don't understand why people who want to die, live and people who want to live, die.

I don't understand why you have to go through pain and disappointments when, in my opinion, you do nothing to warrant the suffering.

I don't understand how eternity in heaven can be a gift—free of charge.

There is much your dad doesn't understand. But I believe the reason I don't understand these things is because God never intended that we understand the complexities of life. He simply wants you and me to have complete faith. All we need to understand is that He is a sovereign God who loves us enough to weave all things, pleasant and unpleasant, together for our good.

Thankfully, there is one thing that I understand perfectly. I understand that you have captured my heart.

Your life has impacted mine immeasurably, and my life would not be complete without you. I carry you and your life's message with me everywhere I go.

One day our Sovereign Father and Friend will allow us to grasp His reasoning. Until then, we must trust Him. He is filled with love for you and me, and He uses the things we don't understand to bring us closer to Him.

God loves you, Lucas, and so do I.

Dad

Chapter Eleven

‚ ‚ ‚ ‚ ‚ ‚ ‚ ‚ ‚ ‚ ‚ ‚ ‚ ‚ ‚ ‚ ‚ ‚ ‚ ‚

Teaching Without Saying a Word

It was Monday morning. I moved quickly down the stairs and into the kitchen where I would eat breakfast with my parents. On this spring day of my high school senior year, our basketball team would face its chief rival in the district semifinals.

We anticipated a difficult game, and my mother was well aware of my competitive nature. As I loaded my duffel bag and headed toward the back door, she stopped me and said, "I want you to know something. I want you to know that tonight you will win. Your team is going to win." I liked this positive attitude, especially from someone who had never played the game of basketball. She exuded confidence that we would defeat one of our toughest competitors despite their talent and season of success. She even reiterated the declaration in order to get her point across. In view of the fact that she knew so little about team records and game strategies, this assurance intrigued me, so I asked why she was so sure that we would have victory.

Without hesitation she replied, "Bob, it's plain and simple. Your opponent practiced on the Sabbath and God will not honor the abuse of His Holy Day. Their team practiced on the Sabbath, so they will lose. Your team didn't, so you will win." Simple. No gray area. No doubt. And the irony was that I believed it completely. As I walked out the door and headed to school, it never occurred to me to question her theory. And we did, indeed, win.

You see, my family, church, and school all taught me the same thing about this cause-and-effect relationship regarding good deeds and bad deeds. The lesson was clear: God rewards those who keep His commandments and punishes those who don't. After all, the Old Testament is full of examples. Chapter 26 of Leviticus says, "If you follow my decrees and are careful to obey my commands, I will send you rain in its season. . . . But if you will not listen to me and carry out all these commands . . . then I will do this to you: I will bring upon you sudden terror, wasting diseases and fever." These words are uncomplicated with little room for misinterpretation. Simple. No gray area. No doubt. Just like Mom.

When Old Testament passages like this merged with an upbringing that reinforced the concept, it's no wonder that the arrival of Lucas caused me to look within. Questions immediately flooded my mind. *What did I do? Why is God choosing to punish me through a son who isn't right?*

Despite many questions, there was one certainty. If God was choosing to use Lucas as some sort of reprimand, then it was definitely meant for me. Not Darla. If you were to study the life of Darla, you would quickly discover that she was deserving of sainthood simply for putting up with me. No, this reproof was not for her. It must have been for me and the result was a serious look in the mirror. What exactly was I being punished for?

As I began to survey my life, one thing became evident. I talked a great talk, but my walk had been very weak. I talked enthusiastically about priorities: God first, then family, then country. It sounded good. It looked good. But a closer look revealed a contradiction. I talked of these priorities, but my walk proved that the pursuit of success received much more energy and attention than God or my family. At the end of the day, winning basketball games was what mattered. Period. I was far more in sync with career advancement than the advancement of God's kingdom or the development of my family.

My life was fast-paced and full-throttle. College was followed by a good teaching job and a head coaching position. At 29 I became a high school principal, despite being one of the youngest staff members at that school. Everything was in gear and life was moving along exactly as planned. So what was the problem? Life had become all about me and not about God.

The conclusion of my life assessment was this: If God had a Leviticus moment and saw the need to send me a message, then the message was clear and the messenger was a son named Lucas. The biggest question that remained was, "Why him?" If I was the one that needed a reality check, why not inflict the harm on me— on my body? Let me suffer ill health. Let me experience the pain of countless needles and a lifetime of dependence on others.

Why not me? Because God knew that I prided myself in being an incredibly strong person, determined to rise above the difficult circumstances of life. He knew that it would take more than the usual two-by-four to get my attention.

God has an intimate knowledge of His children and is fully aware of the exact circumstance that will bring us to complete reliance on Him. He knew that Lucas was the very "thing" that would bring me to my knees quickly. I was completely helpless. I couldn't change a thing. I couldn't make him right, and the guilt was relentless. Was Lucas meant to be a punishment for my poor choices? If I had been more responsible or more spiritual, would he have been born healthy?

Jesus responded to a similar question in John 9:1-3, and His answer has given me great solace. Jesus and His followers happen upon a blind man, and the disciples ask, "Who sinned, this man or his parents, that he was born blind?" After all, the disciples had received the very same Old Testament teaching I had: Infirmity is the result of bad behavior.

At this point I imagine Jesus might simply smile, knowing they just don't get it. He answers them gently, "Neither this man nor his parents sinned . . . but this happened so that the work of God might be displayed in his life." The reason this man was born with a disability was so the work of God might be displayed in his life.

Reflecting on this story has helped me to sincerely thank God for Lucas. It gives me great comfort to say, "No one sinned." When Jesus made that statement, He was not declaring that the man or his parents were sinless. He was affirming that human inadequacies are purposeful and the challenges of life are not necessarily the result of our sins. Instead, our challenges and infirmities offer opportunities for God to reveal His mercy and grace. He knows full well that we all have sinned and fallen short of His glory (Romans 3:23).

Before Lucas was born, God knew every sin I ever committed and every bad choice I ever made, and yet He forgave me. He knows your every sin, and yet He chose to die for you. His love for me, for Lucas, and for you is so great that while we were still sinners, He died for us (Romans 5:8). There is great freedom in acknowledging our imperfections and great power in embracing the cross.

Thousands of years ago Jesus revealed the purpose for Lucas's life with a few words. Our son was not brought into this world as a punishment for anyone's sin but to be a reflection of God's wonder, an instrument of God's mercy, and a catalyst to make me more like Christ. Through his human frailty, Lucas has inspired the competent and challenged the strong. A close family friend once described how Lucas has been used in her life to reveal the character of God:

> He is full of joy, peace, patience (most of the time), kindness, goodness, gentleness, and he exudes unconditional love. He isn't impressed with a person's worldly status, doesn't care much about receiving things, and isn't mindful of what others think of him. He just loves for me to spend time with him, holding him and singing to him. We could literally sit for hours doing just that, and he would be genuinely content, clapping his hands with a smile on his face. People always say that the eyes are a window to the soul—I see that in Lucas. It doesn't matter if he's healthy, happy, tired, sick, or hurting, I always see Jesus revealed in him.

This testimony is a powerful reminder to me of the irony that Lucas is not a punishment for poor choices, but a messenger of God's love. Though poor choices will almost certainly result in negative consequences, when we accept the gift of grace Jesus offers us, we are no longer condemned. The Old Testament law existed to reveal human weakness, to reveal the need for a Savior, but there is now no condemnation for those who are in Christ Jesus (Romans 8:1). The new life Christ offers is not about keeping track of good deeds and bad deeds, hoping the good stuff comes out ahead. It is about realizing our weaknesses, accepting His love and forgiveness, and working diligently to become more like Him.

As we have walked this journey with Lucas, I have often reflected on the life of Job. Job was a good man, blameless and upright, a man who feared God and shunned evil (Job 1:8). His life was full of good deeds, right priorities, and great wealth, yet God allowed him to be tested through unthinkable loss. His material possessions were destroyed, all of his children and most of his servants were killed, and his body was inflicted with painful sores from the soles of his feet to the top of his head.

Sitting in a heap of ashes, the only comfort he received from his wife was the recommendation that he give up his integrity, curse God, and die! Job had no one to blame and nothing to hope for. Just as I questioned myself and my integrity when Lucas was born, Job began asking God to show him what sin he had committed to deserve such incredible catastrophe. He asked God why he was ever born and why he should go on living.

God listened patiently as Job tried to make sense of his situation, and then God responded with a few questions of His own in chapters 38-40:

> Who is this that darkens my counsel with words without knowledge? . . . Where were you when I laid the earth's foundation? . . . What is the way to the place where the lightning is dispersed? . . . Can you bring forth the constellations in their seasons? . . . Does the hawk take flight by your wisdom . . . [or] the eagle soar at your command and build his nest on high? . . . Do you have an arm like God's, and can your voice thunder like his? Then adorn yourself with glory and splendor, and clothe yourself in honor and majesty . . . then I myself will admit to you that your own right hand can save you.

This reproach brought Job to a position of utter humility. "Surely I spoke of things I did not understand. . . . My ears had heard of you but now my eyes have seen you" (Job 42:3, 5).

Prior to Lucas, I too spoke of things I did not understand. My life was about image—looking good and sounding good. I was raised in a Christian home, attended church twice every Sunday, lived in a Christian community, went to a Christian high school, and graduated from a Christian college. I knew Scripture from memory and heard the stories of the Bible countless times.

My knowledge was abundant but I lacked understanding. Lucas was a catalyst to my enlightenment. The helplessness I experienced taught me to humble myself before God and man. Becoming aware of my sinfulness taught me I would never be good enough to deserve God's love or bad enough to lose it.

My ears had heard of the Lord, but it was the gift of Lucas that opened my eyes to really see Him. It was the gift of Lucas that personalized God's sovereignty and grace, and it was the gift of Lucas that made me realize basketball games are not what truly matter. At the end of the day, what truly matters is becoming more like Christ.

Seeing God work through the life of Lucas has produced far more wisdom than years of hearing. He cannot recite Scripture or inspire others with eloquent words, but his message has been loud and clear. His quiet lessons have caused the following poem to become very dear to me:

> I'd rather see a sermon than hear one any day;
> I'd rather one should walk with me than merely tell the way.
> The eye's a better pupil and more willing than the ear,
> Fine counsel is confusing, but example's always clear . . .[9]

The situations and events of our lives will shout to the deepest part of our souls louder than any speech or sermon. My mind had been filled with good and true information. God knew that a lecture on priorities or His grace and sovereignty would simply be filed in the archives of my mind, but He knew that Lucas would teach me things that would change the way I lived.

I suppose you could say that Lucas has been my sermon—and he has delivered it powerfully without ever saying a word.

Dear Lucas,

The number "13" has become very special to me because it represents you. It's the day you were born—June 13.

Many people consider the number "13" to represent bad luck. Many builders of skyscrapers skip the number "13" when numbering their floors, believing too many guests would be uncomfortable staying or doing business on the 13th floor.

There was a time when I kind of bought into that logic. Not anymore! I view June 13 as a special day and, therefore, the number "13" has become a perfect reminder of the gift God gave us in you.

Most mornings I set my alarm clock for 6:13 A.M. The numbers "6-13" remind me to give my best for the day, because I know you have to give your best every day. Many times your brothers will yell out "6-13" when the numbers come on our television or on our car radio. They too give thanks for you. In fact, "6-13" is an active and constant reminder to our whole family to pray for you and to give God thanks for you.

I don't take little things like eating, reading, writing, running, talking, and driving for granted. These are things I get to do every day, and it is your life that encourages me to invest these abilities for maximum daily impact.

When I have to wake up earlier, I set the alarm in a

sequence of numbers that add up to 13 or with the minutes that end in 13. For example, many times I will set the alarm for 5:26 A.M.—*five plus two plus six equals thirteen.* And again I think of you. Or, I'll set the alarm for 7:13 A.M. because the number ends in 13, and again I think of you.

This ritual may seem silly to some, but it has become a significant part of my day, calling me to a higher standard each morning.

My day starts better when I think of you, and that puts things in right focus before my feet ever touch the floor. It is your life of perseverance, your competitive spirit, and your unconditional love that motivate me to strive for authenticity and make a difference in the lives of others.

You inspire me, kid. And you do it without saying a word!

Dad

Chapter Twelve

♦ ♦ ♦ ♦ ♦ ♦ ♦ ♦ ♦ ♦ ♦ ♦ ♦ ♦ ♦ ♦ ♦ ♦ ♦ ♦

Trust in the Midst of the Storm

Reflections from a mother's heart by Darla Vander Plaats

Our morning was off to a routine start as Lucas and I drove the rural highways between our home and one of the many medical facilities that provided him care and therapy.

We were usually joined by three-year-old Josh, chattering the whole way, but today it was just Lucas and me. And I was soaking up the rare moments of silence in the van.

Lucas was still an infant and his car seat was positioned in its usual place, nestled between the two front seats on the floor. Although its placement didn't comply with safety standards, it was necessary for us. Lucas never went long without needing assistance, and I had to be able to reach him easily and quickly.

For the moment Lucas was asleep, and in the quiet of my mind I began to consider the strange and frightening turns my life had taken over the past several months. I began experiencing mental, emotional, and physical "turns" the moment Lucas was born, and the stress of it was more than an occasional sensation or an overused cliché. For me, it had become a lifestyle.

There was emotional stress. I grieved for the child we had

planned and hoped for, knowing Lucas would never fit our original expectations. I never asked for or planned on a child with so many problems and never envisioned the kind of lifestyle that Lucas brought with him. It wasn't long before I began viewing myself in a whole new way. I had become "the mother of a disabled child," as if it was the most defining thing about my entire life, and emotionally that was difficult to accept.

With much grief came much guilt, and the stress of it continued to build. Early on Bob and I didn't realize that the feelings we fought were part of an acceptable and even necessary process. Instead, the guilt churned within us, suggesting that we didn't love the "imperfect" child we had been given. And it was something neither of us talked about.

There was mental stress. I had so much to learn in such a short time. Literally overnight, we were expected to know a flood of medical terms and procedures. We began working with a branch of the public school system that dealt with the special needs of children like Lucas, learning about Individual Education Plans, early interventions, and processes I had never heard of before.

In addition to tracking the scheduling demands of in-home appointments, hospital and doctor visits, medication needs, and therapy routines throughout the day, I was determined to remain fully attentive to the many joys and demands of our two healthy sons, who desperately needed me. My mind was in a constant spin cycle.

There was financial stress. The responsibility of handling the family budget wasn't a serious stress to me, being the accountant of the family, but our financial situation was similar to that of many young families. Bob was the primary breadwinner, still getting established in his career and experiencing many moves and changes along the way. We had moved just months before Lucas was born and were still adjusting to a new set of financial circumstances. Now, having a child with severe disabilities was a new financial stress for us to deal with, one that included insurance deductibles and co-pays, increased travel for medical appointments, and hospitalizations which led to hotel and restaurant bills.

We encountered the need for nutritional supplements, which were not the least of our newfound expenses. The good news was that the added nutrients and calories helped Lucas maintain his weight and seemed to make him much more content. The bad news was that the stuff was expensive! Our insurance didn't cover nutritional supplements even if prescribed by a doctor, so our grocery budget took a hit.

There was physical stress. My days were consumed with maintaining our home, giving piano lessons, caring for Lucas and the rest of the family, and playing taxi driver. To be completely honest, it was often a strange sort of relief when Lucas was hospitalized, because then I had the help of wonderful nurses and health-care aides. They took care of Lucas while I was forced to let the rest of my duties go. I could just sit and cross-stitch, read, or sleep. They were rare moments of solitude, to say the least.

At home it was go, go, go all day long, and the nights were rarely restful. Even when Lucas was feeling well, which wasn't often, he would wake up several times a night. When he was sick, I either bedded down in his room beside the crib or just held him in my arms while trying to catch a few moments of sleep in the recliner. All of this was exhausting enough, but what really sapped my energy was wondering if it would ever let up. As I looked ahead to the coming days, weeks, months, and years, I feared exhaustion would become my permanent condition.

The height of stress for me came from trying to act as though everything was fine. Maybe I wasn't covering nearly as well as I thought, but I felt pressured to wear a mask of composed competence. I tried to act as if nothing had really changed in my life, as if our family was no different from friends' or siblings' families. I had everything under control. But this confident facade was nothing more than a thin covering over insecurity and anger lurking just beneath the surface.

In that private place, driving the rolling highways, an emotional storm began to brew. *Why me? Why my child? Why my family? What is going to happen? How am I going to keep doing this?* On and on the questions pounded, and my feelings of grief, disappointment, helplessness, and fear were met with no immediate relief.

Most of the time when such painful questions surfaced, I simply shoved them to the back of my mind until the chaos of life swept them away. But at that moment, when the only thing begging for attention was the very storm I was trying to avoid, it all washed over me and I was completely overwhelmed.

Romans 8:26 says, "We do not know what we ought to pray for, but the Spirit himself intercedes for us with groans that words cannot express." If the truth of that verse ever applied to me, it was at that moment. In the midst of turmoil, God answered a prayer I didn't even know how to pray by sending His Spirit to minister to my spirit in a powerful way. I had never experienced anything like it.

God began revealing precious and simple truths that brought healing to my wounded heart and peace to my tired mind. For the first time in months, I became aware of how much I had to be thankful for.

Even though our financial condition wasn't ideal, it was also not terrible, and I began to realize how blessed we were to have good medical insurance that prevented us from accumulating the devastating medical debt burdening other families in our situation. Feelings of frustration began turning into feelings of gratitude.

Once He had my attention, the Lord began showing me some things about my marriage. Bob was incredibly busy during those years, working hard to establish his career as a high school principal, and I never questioned his commitment to either his career or his family. Sheldon High School, where he served, had some sort of activity scheduled nearly every night. From sporting events to music concerts, Bob was there for it all. He was absorbed in doing his job well, and the students and teachers loved him.

I wanted him to succeed. I was proud of his accomplishments, and I knew that he was having a positive effect on many lives. So why did it bother me? It bothered me because every time he headed out the door to an event, I was left home alone to care for our three little boys and manage the details of our family. He loved me and was a loving father to the boys, but when the boys were young—before the basketball years—I longed for him to be a more hands-on father.

Part of me understood that it was the most efficient and effective arrangement, to let him worry about his job and provide financial stability while I worried about the details of our home. It had worked well for us so far. In the meantime, I was starting to question whether it was really the best way, now that we had Lucas. Resentment grew as I witnessed Bob's good nights of sleep. He felt it was necessary in order to be effective at his job, and I felt it was a built-in excuse to be removed from the reality of our situation.

Thankfully, in the quiet moments of revelation, God showed me a new picture of my husband. Bob had become my strong, dependable safety net. I was out there walking a tightrope, day by day, but I didn't have any real fear of falling because I knew without a doubt, Bob would be there to catch me if things fell apart.

He would be there to pick me up and put me back on my feet. I took a hard look at what life would be like without him as my supporter, helper, and friend. Again I was moved to tears of gratitude.

Little did I know, as Lucas and I headed to the doctor that morning, that I was the one in need of healing. God shifted my focus in a significant way that day, and for the first time in months I recognized what was right with my life rather than focusing on what was wrong. My circumstances had not changed during the 50-minute drive, but my heart had come full circle, and my feelings of loss were replaced with an attitude of abundance.

Without a doubt the healing touch of God was at work within me, and if I had ever doubted His transforming power, I never would again. Praise God from whom all blessings flow!

Of course, God never stops working in our hearts, and He still had work to do in mine. With newfound inner peace and stability, my compassion grew for those who were experiencing similar emotional bondage. Suddenly I was aware that Bob and I had a beautiful opportunity, if we were willing, to use our story to reach out to others.

In chapters 42-50 of Genesis, Joseph comes face-to-face with the brothers who beat him, stripped him of his clothes, and sold him into slavery. If anyone had the right to resent his life-circumstances, it was Joseph—and nobody would have blamed him for it. But Joseph looked into his brothers' eyes and said, "You intended to harm me, but God intended it for good to accomplish what is now being done, the saving of many lives" (Genesis 50:20). Joseph chose to focus on the good instead of the bad and because he did, God used him to touch the lives of many.

There is much debate in our society about babies like Lucas, whether their lives have value or not. The birth of Lucas caused me feelings of anger and disappointment, and I found myself stuck in the stress of it for months, unwilling to see beyond my own discomfort. As difficult as it is to admit, there were times in those early months when I did question the life of Lucas. I loved him, but I wondered what purpose God could possibly have for him.

Thankfully, God began to reveal His purpose for Lucas over and over again. It became wonderfully clear that God was choosing to use our "tragedy" for good, both in our lives and in the lives of others. But before God could make His purpose clear to me, I had to stop fighting my circumstances, stop trying to change them, and simply submit to His will. I had to trust that He knew best, that His plan was much better than mine could ever be. I had to put Lucas in His hands, and trust Him to use our family as He saw fit.

I imagine the storm raging inside me during the months following Lucas's birth was much like the storm Jesus and His disciples encountered on the Sea of Galilee waves crashing over the sides of the boat, lightning flashing, thunder booming, confusion and panic all around. But there was no panic for Jesus. In the midst of chaos, Jesus simply rebuked the storm and the storm stopped. It was no more miraculous in the lives of the disciples thousands of years ago than it was when God calmed the storm in my heart, driving the highways of northwest Iowa.

I will always treasure the moments Bob and I shared when Lucas and I returned home that evening. For the first time, we talked—really talked—about the presence of Lucas in our lives, and we began to grasp the idea that God was going to turn something that seemed tragic into something more beautiful than either of us could have ever imagined. We found our bearings. We found new purpose and new meaning. Most importantly, we began to trust.

Of course, there have been struggles since then. Lucas was not healed; life did not become easy. But the storm in my heart has not come back. Through medical emergencies, sleepless nights, disappointments, and separations, the peace that passes all understanding prevails when I remember the day God calmed my storm.

Though the journey so far has been very different from what I imagined when I first learned we were expecting our third child, I know now that God's plan is perfect even when my circumstances aren't.

"For I know the plans I have for you," declares the LORD, "plans to prosper you and not to harm you, plans to give you hope and a future. Then you will call upon me and come and pray to me, and I will listen to you. You will seek me and find me when you seek me with all your heart" (Jeremiah 29:11-13).

God is waiting for us to cry out to Him in our pain and fear and frustration. He desperately wants us to seek Him in the midst of our storm so He can prove Himself faithful. There is no judgment. There is no condemnation. There is no, "Are you kidding me?" There is simply grace and hope, and the wonderful knowledge that we can trust Him completely because He loves us perfectly.

A LETTER TO LUCAS, FROM MOM

My Little Lucilon,

I still call you that even though you are hardly little anymore. You've grown so much physically and yet remain so sweet and gentle, innocent and untouched by this world. How wonderful it would be if we could all be more like you.

You need so little to be content: a full tummy, dry clothes, a warm bed (but not too warm), music, and several catnaps a day. When these basic needs are met, you are truly

*happy. Add in some individual attention from family mem-
bers or Ruth, and your cup overflows!*

*Yes, maintaining your health is complicated, but your
life is simple. Most of the things that seem so important to
the rest of us, things that we chase after and fret about,
mean nothing to you. You've got life whittled down to the
basics: physical needs and positive, undemanding, uncomplicated relationships with people. The rest of it simply
doesn't exist in your world.*

*All of that leads me to the most important thing I've
learned from you: the reality that I can trust God in this life
while He prepares me for the next. You are a constant living
reminder that this world is not where we belong, and you're
a beautiful example of what it means to be in the world,
but not of the world. I think we both know that we're not
experiencing the kind of life God intended when He first
created the earth. Sure, there is beauty and joy in this life,
but there is also pain and sadness. It's all intertwined. Most
every moment of joy is tinged with a measure of sadness,
and oftentimes we find ourselves surprised by the presence of
beauty in the midst of our saddest days.*

*We live in a fallen world, but we are blessed with
glimpses of God's grace. Your life has provided many of those
glimpses and has made me long for the day when we will
experience our Father's best—together.*

*On that day, I will become more like you than you will
become like me. You will shed your physical limitations and
live pain-free. You will be able to communicate and express
your every thought and idea. But I will also be transformed.
I will shed the cares and concerns of this world and live as*

purely as you. I can't wait until I am given the ability to love people as sweetly as you do, experience joy as unhindered as you do, and trust as completely as you do.

Thank you for the wonderful gift you have given me, Lucas—a peek into eternity. I love you!

Mom

Chapter Thirteen

Unconditional Love

The chapters and words of this book sprung from my love for Lucas and a passion to assist him in fulfilling his life's purpose: motivating "normal" people to live extraordinary lives. I sincerely hope this "light from Lucas" will inspire and challenge you to live your one-and-only life to its fullest, in red-hot pursuit of your purpose.

The ultimate conclusion of the light I have gleaned from Lucas is and always has been unconditional love. The mere existence of Lucas continually reveals the fundamental nature of love . . . love without condition.

I love Lucas and Lucas loves me. We love each other without strings and without expectations—just pure, untainted love between a son and his dad. It is said that love is the greatest gift. I believe that's true. The reason Lucas has been such a precious gift is because he has brought so much love to our lives.

Our world seems to be in a constant struggle to grasp the concept of "true love." We use the term so casually it has nearly lost its significance. Though we easily express love and affection for our favorite sports teams, foods, articles of clothing, and vehicles, we find it difficult to express our love for one another.

There are many grown men and women who still long to hear the words "I love you" from their parents, and there are many moms and dads who long to hear these words from their children.

How can such a simple task be so difficult? I believe it's difficult because it involves risk.

When crossing the "I love you" line, we enter uncharted territory and our minds begin playing games. "What happens if they don't say 'I love you' back?" asks the doubter. "She already knows I love her, so why must I express it?" reminds the realist. So why do we need to express it? It is simple. We need to say "I love you" because the people in our lives need to know they are loved.

More than 30,000 people commit suicide each year in the United States.[10] I believe this disheartening statistic exists because people have a love-void. Children are having children. Teens and adults alike are having random sex in search of love, only to find emptiness and disappointment.

Expressing genuine, appropriate love for one another is vital to growing healthy relationships. For many, expressing love is something foreign, a job they simply don't know how to do. So let's explore the most basic ways to communicate love.

The first and most straightforward option for communicating your love is to simply say it. "I love you." These three little words, when authentically uttered, break down walls, fill gaps, and provide the basis for healing and growth. Go ahead—you can do it! Say the words to your children, your mom and dad, your friends and relatives, and anyone else who needs to know you love him or her.

Once you have said it, write it. We all enjoy receiving written communication from someone special. Whether expressed by a handwritten note, an e-mail, a text message, or a formal letter, the written word is incredibly meaningful and can be preserved for generations.

Any time I receive a note of encouragement I file it in an "I'm okay" folder. Thus, when bad days come and people are unkind, I can open the file drawer, remove both notes (kidding!), and read them as a reminder that someone loves me.

Say it. Write it. Now say "I love you" with a touch. There are times when a pat on the back, an embrace, a gentle squeeze of the neck, or holding someone's hand communicates more effectively than words ever could. I have resorted to touch many times simply because I didn't know what to say. A timely touch can say, "I'm here and I care."

In John 13:1-5, Jesus says "I love you" by demonstrating humility:

> It was just before the Passover Feast. Jesus knew that the time had come for him to leave this world and go to the Father. Having loved his own who were in the world, he now showed them the full extent of his love.
>
> The evening meal was being served, and the devil had already prompted Judas Iscariot, son of Simon, to betray Jesus. Jesus knew that the Father had put all things under his power, and that he had come from God and was returning to God; so he got up from the meal, took off his outer clothing, and wrapped a towel around his waist. After that, he poured water into a basin and began to wash his disciples' feet, drying them with the towel that was wrapped around him.

Notice the words, "He now showed them the full extent of his love." Jesus taught many lessons, performed many miracles, and displayed many acts of kindness. Here He humbled Himself to wash the feet of His disciples.

Communicating genuine love requires a certain amount of

humility. This may be the reason our twenty-first-century world has such difficulty expressing unconditional love. Humility is contrary to pop culture. We have been taught to hold our heads high and take pride in ourselves so we will appear strong to others. Humility, on the other hand, may be thought of as weak.

Christ is all-powerful, able to wake the dead with a simple command, yet He took on the role of a servant in order to prove His love. Many of us need to humble ourselves and symbolically or physically wash the feet of the people we love. If Jesus could do it, though He was without fault, surely we can do it.

Our God-given emotions can also express love beautifully. Paul tells us in Romans 12:15, "Rejoice with those who rejoice; mourn with those who mourn." Great love is expressed when we sincerely celebrate the blessings of others or weep with those who experience pain. Our culture, especially the world of politics, teaches us to cheer inside when others experience difficulty and envy the blessings they receive, but Scripture is clear that we are to truly desire the best for others. Our emotions are a powerful component of our internal love-gauge.

My final suggestion in this not-all-inclusive list of ways to show love is to forgive. Ephesians 4:32 says, "Be kind and compassionate to one another, forgiving each other, just as in Christ God forgave you." Many relational pains arise as a result of unforgiving, bitter hearts, but Scripture reminds us that we are all in need of forgiveness. We must let go of injustice and move on.

When I was serving as a high school principal, two of my female students were involved in a nasty fight—punching, pulling, tearing, yelling, and crying. After some cool-down time, I called them into my office in an attempt to discover the cause of such cruelty between friends. I learned the fight and emotion that fueled the punches were due to a remark that had been made in the sixth grade! The remark, as I recall, was one girl telling the other that she looked bad in a bathing suit.

I sat there dumbfounded. Here were two high school juniors, fighting over a remark made some five years earlier. Now I was the one with the pleasure of disciplining them for something that should have been resolved long ago. Give it up already!

If this were an isolated incident, it could be a bit comical, but the sad commentary is that many adults are still suffering from comments or actions of long ago, simply because they are unwilling to humble themselves and offer or ask for forgiveness. Paul tells us to forgive each other as Christ forgave us. In other words, we don't deserve forgiveness, but Christ forgives us anyway.

Go ahead—forgive those who have hurt you, then write and tell me of your newfound freedom!

Whether you choose to express your love by saying, writing, touching, serving, rejoicing, weeping, or forgiving, just be sure to express it genuinely and without condition. For this is the true measure of love.

Lucas is limited in his ability to express love. He cannot write love notes or say the words "I love you," and he certainly cannot wash the feet of those he loves. Even so, he is quite capable of expressing emotion through the sounds he makes. I love his sounds. Through them Lucas verbalizes happiness, anger, sadness, excitement—and even love. His sounds of "ooh" and "aah" may seem meaningless to others, but they are priceless to me. They are priceless because they are authentic. Every noise Lucas makes comes straight from his heart.

I have had the opportunity to hear many speakers and have given many speeches, but the best speeches, without question, are those that come from the heart. It is a great pleasure to hear someone who can move an audience from laughter to tears back to laughter, and then to reflection and action. It is a talent to be sure, but these speeches only have impact because they come from the heart.

Even though I love to sing, my family is quick to point out my lack of singing talent. I fully realize that singing is not in my area of giftedness. My family, however, will also point out that when I sing, I sing from the heart. It may not make me sound better, but it enhances their tolerance and makes people smile.

"Heart" inspires people. A vocalist may give a technically perfect performance, but if it lacks spirit, it is nothing more than notes on a page. Inspiration comes when a singer combines extraordinary talent with a heart of passion.

First Corinthians 13:1 says, "If I speak in the tongues of men and of angels, but have not love, I am only a resounding gong or a clanging cymbal." In other words, talk is cheap. Words are just words unless they come from the heart.

Lucas is not articulate by the world's standards. But, the messages of love he expresses through indistinct sounds are often more powerful than those of the best-trained preacher using the most eloquent words.

Love and passion are the motivator and activator of the message!

Unfortunately the world we live in has too many ways of defining love, most of which are grossly distorted and untrue. These misuses and exploitations of "love" contrast with Lucas's refreshing authenticity. There is not an inauthentic bone in his body. In fact it would never occur to Lucas to use his affections to manipulate others or to be self-indulgent when it comes to love.

When I have the opportunity to address parents of teenagers, I remind them that boys will give "love" as a means to get sex, while girls will give sex as a means to get "love." The message is clear and simple. Parents of daughters, make certain your little girl knows you love her—authentically. Parents of boys, make sure that your son understands and respects the true meaning and source of love.

This age-old battle between the worldly exploitation of love and love's divine intention is quite possibly the "tipping point" between a life of purpose and a life of wasted potential. It boils down to a matter of focus. People can choose to focus their talents and gifts on personal satisfaction or on benefiting others. The decisions we make about how to use our abilities stem directly from a focus of the heart.

The focus of God's heart is perfectly clear: "For God so loved the world that he gave his one and only Son, that whoever believes in him shall not perish but have eternal life" (John 3:16). God has one Son, Jesus. He chose Jesus, who is without sin, to bear the sins of the world so you and I could have eternal life in heaven. God's heart is focused on us, the prize of His creation.

God has one Son. I have four. I believe I have a heart for others, yet I cannot begin to think about sending one of my sons to his death for the faults of others. Whether or not I can comprehend it, Christ says this is how we are to love. Before He departed this earth He said, "A new command I give you: Love one another. As I have loved you, so you must love one another. By this all men will know that you are my disciples" (John 13:34-35). Christ was ridiculed, beaten, and put to death for us. Can God be serious?

Yes, God is serious.

He wants us to die to ourselves and to live for Him. If that means ridicule, beatings, disabilities, or even death, so be it. Life on earth is temporary. Life with Christ is eternal. It's a matter of heart.

Love's true meaning provides me much comfort regarding the life and purpose of Lucas.

Lucas is patient—through needles, surgeries, seizures, the awkward stares of strangers, and constant poking and prodding that is so often necessary for his care.

Lucas is kind—readily giving second chances and smiling in spite of the sometimes-inadequate efforts of those he depends upon.

Lucas does not envy or boast, and he is not proud. Lucas is Lucas. His humble life encapsulates love, because the purpose of his life is for the benefit of others, not himself.

Lucas is not easily angered and he keeps no record of wrongs. Lucas has every right, according to the world's standards, to be angry, to have pity parties, and to hold people's actions against them. Instead, he claps his chest and screams through a tracheotomy tube that he loves life and those around him. When I observe Lucas's resilient behavior, I have to ask, "What's my problem?"

Lucas does not delight in evil but rejoices with the truth, bringing out the best in people: doctors, caregivers, brothers, casual bystanders, and his mom and dad.

Lucas always protects—displaying his love and joy for family, special friends, and those responsible for his care. His facial expressions and physical behavior never depict a boy who has been cheated by life. Instead, his face says, "Thanks for loving me."

Lucas always trusts. Wow, does he ever! He has to trust. He is fully dependent for nourishment, personal care, and his overall well-being. His life has been built on trust. Because of the special love Christ showed those with special needs while on earth, I believe Lucas knows and trusts his risen Savior and sovereign God in a very personal way.

Lucas always hopes—to walk, run, and talk. I am confident his hopes will be realized when he meets Jesus face-to-face. In heaven every one of Lucas's tears will be wiped away and every disability restored. Darla and I long to see him in heaven—what a day that will be!

Lucas always perseveres. Many doctors have given us reasons for Lucas to give up on life, but Lucas has continually shown an incredible will to live. He has persevered through seizures, through needles, through conspicuous stares, and through his daily, routine obstacles. His perseverance motivates me to keep striving!

First Corinthians 13:10 says, "But when perfection comes, the imperfect disappears." Jesus Christ is perfect. This world is imperfect; you, me, a multitude of sins, and even the pain of Lucas's disabilities. God sent His perfect Son to save a world burdened with defects.

When I picture Christ on the cross with His arms outstretched, I see the heart of our Father God saying, "I love you this much." When I stop to consider the powerful impact Lucas has had on my life, I can hear God saying, "I love you this much."

The greatest expression of love is accepting Jesus Christ as our personal Lord and Savior. By accepting this great gift, we experience the absolute love of our Creator. Our response to the Father's love should be a life committed to Him, to His will, and to the advancement of His kingdom. And the most excellent way to show our love for the Father is to love those He has brought into our lives.

I believe Lucas was created to reveal God's love and glory, and I praise God for giving Darla, our boys, and me the gift of Lucas. We love him and he loves us, unconditionally.

Lucas has helped me understand unconditional love, and for this I am eternally grateful. Through many years and many tears, I have loved Lucas just as he is. I don't know what tomorrow will bring, but I have faith and hope in our Lord to carry our family through. And I have a precious and powerful love for Lucas that can never be taken away.

"Now these three remain: faith, hope and love. But the greatest of these is love" (1 Corinthians 13:13).

Afterword

Lucas and I just finished an early morning cruise. I enjoyed my coffee and he enjoyed his ride in the Suburban. He is doing so well. When I sing to him, he tilts his head back and frames his mouth with his hands as if holding a note to join in the singing. I love it when he does that. He actually likes to listen to his dad sing!

He squints, wrinkles, and coos when I talk to him, joining in the conversation. He is a great young man who continues to bless me, Darla, our family, and others with his presence. Through many moments of medical uncertainty we have wondered if Lucas would live to be a teenager. I'm proud to say that upon publication of this book, Lucas is 13 years old and full of more joy and life than ever before. The simple courage with which he lives continues to be an inspiration and we are so thankful for every day we have with him.

When we named him, we weren't aware that Lucas's name derives from the word "light," but it seems a perfect fit for the boy who has brought light into so many lives.

Through Lucas, God continues to soften my heart and open my eyes to the many emotional and physical needs of families and individuals affected by disabilities. Lucas has awakened a passion in me to honor such people, helping them experience the best possible quality of life and celebrate every moment they have here on earth.

Darla and I are excited to be working with an organization in our community to build a state-of-the-art camp for people with disabilities, a place where campers of all ages and abilities can participate in challenging activities and experience success.

Hiking, canoeing, and horseback riding should not be reserved for the "normal." Camp High Hopes will provide extraordinary opportunities for extraordinary boys and girls, men and women.[11]

I know God is pleased when a young man with Down syndrome laughs wildly while catching his first fish, or a woman confined to a wheelchair is able to climb a tree for the first time in her life! These are His children, just like you and me, and He wants them to enjoy the world He created.

Darla and I would love to have you join us on this life's journey. Look around you. There are people with disabilities in your town and in your neighborhood who need friends. There are moms and dads of disabled children who need an encouraging word or a helping hand.

We never imagined, 13 years ago, what God had in store for our family. Lucas will never be the basketball player I expected, but he has become so much more. He has become my hero and, as long as we're together, Lucas will be teaching and I will be learning.

Thank you for sharing this glimpse into our lives. I pray that the story of Lucas has blessed you, and you will find new inspiration to face your days with a little more faith, a little more hope, and a lot more love.

Notes

1. *Off the Practice Field . . . Coach Lou Holtz.* University of Notre Dame. November 5, 1986. <http://und.cstv.com/sports/m-footbl/archive/96season/nd-game08/nd-m-fb-ev-gm08-ccon.html> Accessed April 25, 2006.
2. *The White House: John Kennedy.* <http://www.whitehouse.gov/history/presidents/jk35.html> April 25, 2006.
3. *Chariots of Fire.* Dir. Hugh Hudson. Twentieth Century Fox, 1981.
4. J.J. Redick. ESPN. February 12, 2005.
5. Rabbi Paysach J. Krohn, *Echoes of the Maggid* (New York: Mesorah Publications, 1999).
6. Patrick Fagan and Robert Rector, *The Effects of Divorce on America.* Heritage Foundation. June 5, 2000. <http://www.heritage.org/Research/Family/BG1373.cfm> April 25, 2006.
7. *Ronald Wilson Reagan: Remarks by Patti Davis.* Ronald Reagan Presidential Foundation. June 5, 2004. <http://www.ronaldreaganmemorial.com/remarks_by_Patti_Davis.asp> April 25, 2006.
8. Johann von Schiller, *World of Quotes* <http://www.worldofquotes.com/author/Johann-Von-Schiller/1/index.html> April 25, 2006.
9. Edgar Guest, *Collected Verse of Edgar Guest* (New York: Buccaneer Books, 1976).

10. *Suicide Facts and Statistics: Suicide Is a Leading Killer in America.* Suicide and Crisis Center. December 1, 2004. <http://www.sccenter.org/facts.html> April 25, 2006.

11. To learn more about Camp High Hopes, visit www.camphighhopes.com.

FOCUS ᴼᴺ THE FAMILY®

Welcome to the family!

Whether you purchased this book, borrowed it, or received it as a gift, we're glad you're reading it. It's just one of the many helpful, encouraging, and biblically based resources produced by Focus on the Family for people in all stages of life.

Focus began in 1977 with the vision of one man, Dr. James Dobson, a licensed psychologist and author of numerous best-selling books on marriage, parenting, and family. Alarmed by the societal, political, and economic pressures that were threatening the existence of the American family, Dr. Dobson founded Focus on the Family with one employee and a once-a-week radio broadcast aired on 36 stations.

Now an international organization reaching millions of people daily, Focus on the Family is dedicated to preserving values and strengthening and encouraging families through the life-changing message of Jesus Christ.

Focus on the Family Magazines

These faith-building, character-developing publications address the interests, issues, concerns, and challenges faced by every member of your family from preschool through the senior years.

| Focus on the Family **Citizen®** U.S. news issues | Focus on the Family **Clubhouse Jr.™** Ages 4 to 8 | Focus on the Family **Clubhouse™** Ages 8 to 12 | **Breakaway®** Teen guys | **Brio®** Teen girls 12 to 16 | **Brio & Beyond®** Teen girls 16 to 19 | **Plugged In®** Reviews movies, music, TV |

FOR MORE INFORMATION

 Online:
Log on to www.family.org
In Canada, log on to www.focusonthefamily.ca

 Phone:
Call toll free: (800) A-FAMILY (232-6459)
In Canada, call toll free: (800) 661-9800

More Great Resources
from Focus on the Family®

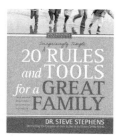

20 (Surprisingly Simple) Rules and Tools for a Great Family
By Dr. Steve Stephens

Creating a great family doesn't have to be difficult or require a lot of hard work. It's really about little changes that produce big results. *20 (Surprisingly Simple) Rules and Tools for a Great Family* includes easy-to-apply principles and tools anyone can use to build closer relationships and create lasting memories.

The Complete Guide to Family Health, Fitness and Nutrition
by Dr. Paul Reisser

Who knows your children's sniffles and sneezes better than you? Now take family care-giving to a whole new level with this comprehensive, easy-to-use reference book. In-depth appendices and reference sections provide the most current and reliable medical information available to help you know when to call the doctor.

Why ADHD Doesn't Mean Disaster
by Dennis Swanberg, Dr. Walt Larimore & Diane Passno

Why ADHD Doesn't Mean Disaster provides a realistic, encouraging perspective from parents who have raised children with ADHD, as well as some who have ADHD themselves. Filled with insights, personal stories and sound medical expertise, this book gives parents facing the challenges of handling ADHD hope that breaks through the hype.

FOR MORE INFORMATION

 Online:
Log on to www.family.org
In Canada, log on to www.focusonthefamily.ca.

 Phone:
Call toll free: (800) A-FAMILY
In Canada, call toll free: (800) 661-9800.

BP06XP1